MW01222334

The Blue Dragonfly

The Blue Dragonfly

healing through poetry

Veronica Eley

First Edition

First Print Run – _____ / 350

Hidden Brook Press
www.HiddenBrookPress.com
writers@HiddenBrookPress.com

Copyright © 2021 Hidden Brook Press
Copyright © 2021 Veronica Eley

All rights for poems revert to the author. All rights for book, layout and design remain with Hidden Brook Press. No part of this book may be reproduced except by a reviewer who may quote brief passages in a review. The use of any part of this publication reproduced, transmitted in any form or by any means, electronic, mechanical, photocopied, recorded or otherwise stored in a retrieval system without prior written consent of the publisher is an infringement of the copyright law.

The Blue Dragonfly: healing through poetry
by Veronica Eley

Editor – Roger Langen
Cover Art – Julia Hacker
Digital adaptation of Cover Art – Christopher Robert Grove
Chapter Icons – TPH Canada (Halifax)
Cover Design – Richard M. Grove
Layout and Design – Richard M. Grove

Typeset in Garamond
Printed and bound in USA
Distributed in USA by Ingram,
            in Canada by Hidden Brook Distribution

Library and Archives Canada Cataloguing in Publication

Title: The blue dragonfly : healing through poetry / Veronica Eley.
Names: Eley, Veronica, author.
Description: Poems.
Identifiers: Canadiana 2021024576X |
            ISBN 9781989786499 (softcover)
Subjects: LCSH: Psychic trauma—Poetry.
Classification: LCC PS8609.L44496 B58 2021 |
            DDC C811/.6—dc23

For my husband

Table of Contents

Part 1   Secret Monsters

Part 2   The Bodhisattva

Part 3 Mother

Give sorrow words. The grief that does not speak
Whispers the o'er fraught heart and bids it break.

— William Shakespeare

If any ask me why —
'Twere easier to die —
Than tell.

— Emily Dickinson

Foreword

The Blue Dragonfly – healing through poetry is the result of a midlife diary that evolved into poetry. As presented here, the process of healing through poetry might also be considered as in the tradition of the *memoir* – an inspired example of the story of 'recovery from trauma.'

The writer's ability to express her personal trauma in words, and to make that psychic injury speak through poetry, becomes a major point of universal interest. Though her wings were slow to form, their transparency and agility is evident in nearly every word. In the title poem, it is the poet, we can say, who skims with *'precision / warlike sounds'* across the canvas of her life, now *'etched like / a Japanese painting'* over a *'pond … still and deep.'*

The poems move through three main stages: injury and illness in *1 Secret Monsters*; intervention (experienced like a miracle) in *2 The Bodhisattva*; forgiveness and transcendence in *3 Mother*. Each of these stages is subdivided into smaller gatherings, with poems arranged in sequence in order to reveal different passages in the context of her journey. The story told in these poems is her own, and though she acknowledges her eventual good fortune, she recognizes the fact that for too many there are *'no paths / through the forest,'* only *'an excruciatingly / lonely space … where shadows are larger than light.'*

* * *

In 2019, the surgeon general of California, Nadine Burke Harris, a pediatrician, identified Adverse Childhood Experience as "the major public health issue of our time." The Centers for Disease Control and Prevention estimates the incidence of ACE among the world's child population at nearly 50%. Childhood trauma is thus strikingly common. The often hidden, individual trauma of children is not to be compared with catastrophic collective trauma, like that of the Uighur re-education camp internee or Rohingya fleeing genocide. But its speechless, private character gives it a special poignancy. Words matter.

As the literature about, and of, trauma increases, so does our understanding. The medical literature indicates a trend toward a range of effective therapies and intervention, and of a consequent reduction in the number of lonely and tormented lives. In the creative literature, by contrast, there may already be trauma fatigue. Some argue that pain is the *blue print* for being. So why cry? One answer may be that manuscripts about previously hidden areas of experience are necessary to help pain make sense. Not everyone has God. Trauma language, moreover, is a form of protest, of a piece with the literatures of critique, resistance, and dissent. Such language is opposed to the practices of power, one of whose chief strategies is camouflage for crimes. As the poet declares in the opening poem of this book, the imperative is to resist one's own invisibility, to *'let them know / you are here.'*

How the poet succeeds in her task is discussed in the Afterword, "Trauma Poetics in *The Blue Dragonfly*." This companion commentary tracks closely to the poems. Poetry and essay together illustrate how creative self-expression reshapes trauma *and* makes it visible: as self-healing for the poet, and as the critical occasion for witness by a sympathetic observer. These processes in poet and reader (patient and therapist) work to effect a transformation.

The poems were first written for the poet alone. As published here, they are, secondarily, a message to her mother and father (since passed) and a testament for her children: a daughter early lost, and two sons on challenging journeys of their own. It is hoped this same message will also be of value to strangers.

Roger Langen, Editor

Acknowledgments

The editor gratefully acknowledges Richard (Tai) Grove of Hidden Brook Press for his support and patience in the evolution of this work. Thanks to John B. Lee, poet, for editorial assistance with the Foreword and Afterword. Readers of the manuscript who provided critical and positive encouragement to the author include Terry and Marsha McDonald, Julia Hacker, Chris Marks, Ramabai Espinet, and one other who wishes to remain anonymous.

The editor thanks the author for providing a manuscript in which no word needed change. The Author's Note, an excerpt from a personal letter, is shared by permission.

About the Cover – Cover image – from an original painting inspired by the text – by artist Julia Hacker, Toronto. Digital adaptation by Christopher Robert Grove.

Photography – Photo reproduction and collage by TPH Canada (Halifax). Photograph 2 (of author, with cats) by Pauline Smith, Halifax.

Website – See www.healthrupoetry.com for discussion of *The Blue Dragonfly* – *healing through poetry* and related themes. Suggestions for further reading appear at the Library tab under the rubrics of Theory, Therapy, and Theatre.

1   Secret Monsters

Pain is the colour of certain events.

– Simone Weil

Prelude

Author's Note

My understanding of myself deepened through the transformative role poetry played in my healing. I became for the first time in my life a fully integrated person.

It was through the accomplishment of my M.Ed. at OISE-UT that I learned to stream *the inner spirit, the unconscious* through journaling. Somehow, *tactile learning* suited me. There was a fluid connection between my soul, brain, pen and paper. I was attracted to a popular, repeated concept of *inside out, outside in* which resulted in 600 poems.

In therapy, I discovered a new perspective on the role of the therapist, as a benevolent presence who was not critical but caring and interactive. Even though I was apprehensive, I learned to view the therapy room as a safe place. I was pleased to be able to share my poetry.

Another insight that has a great deal of meaning for me is the role of the witness, who authenticates that feelings and events actually took place and were not just the ramblings of an unstable woman in a world not grounded in reality. Society still does disregard mental over physical maladies.

I am thankful for help in my acquisition of health.

Veronica Eley

a child's tea party

everything was ready
the table, the chairs
neatly arranged
rabbit had his chair
snake his
all but me

the cups, saucers, plates
neatly placed
they had forgotten
I was coming
you know that invisible
feeling

the conspiracy
a hole in my heart
lost and forgotten
before even conceived
and remembered

bang down the cup
on the table
let them know
you are here

grey blanket

earliest memory
driving along
a country road
in the back seat
wrapped
in a grey blanket
in the dark

separation
the side bars
on the hospital bed
two years old
pneumonia

fifteen-year old girl
raped
police declare
emotionally disturbed
wrapped
in a grey blanket
taken home

disturbed
turbulent
the waters
the waves, the waves
are big, mommy
the cold, grey ocean
is deep
I lean against the railing
of the White Star Cunard liner
seven years old

railings
grey blanket
grey, grey

rain on the tin roof

the hardwood corridor that shone
was the labour of the girls
in the Home of the Guardian Angel

I walked down this hall
with a swaddled newborn
in my arms
there was a ritualistic
passing of the baby
in this institution run
by the Sisters of Charity

the walls narrowed
the floor sank
my heart, my heart

an unnatural negotiation
was about to occur
a newborn child
removed from her mother

in my 8th and 9th month of pregnancy
I was employed as a nanny
for Dorothy and Gerard Murphy
they lived
in a lovely stone cottage with a tin roof
I was not good with kids
so I became the cook
Gerard liked garlic on everything
so he was called Garlic Murphy

when it rained
it hammered on the tin roof
horses' hooves pounding on the track
the surf crashing
in and out
the recurring beat of a drum

this was the soundtrack
for the birth of my first child
who I unconsciously called
Veronica, 'true image'

on adoption she was
renamed Krista

memory loss

my memory
fades
in degrees
like
a stone
skipping backwards
over a pond
a migration
of Canada geese
in reverse
a nameless child

I wander
from room
to room
losing objects
as I go

layers
of memory loss
like the crust
of the earth
the erosion
of a
river bank
a rainforest
in distress

I reconstruct
the past
putting on
protective lenses
to avoid
sharp
flying objects

pieces
reconstructed
by medication
bipolar disease
who am I?
the past?
the present?

white angels

my head
fills the room
is a room
my skull
no longer
shields my thoughts
the fortress, my ribs
is shattered

my life
is a room
that I have lived in
too long
saints and angels
protect me
from spilling
this cup of blood
ecstasy, blood, energy

the saints
wear blue
the angels
wear white

Childhood

tortured words

mother couldn't sleep
doing dishes at 7 a.m.
listening to Scottish music

we lived in a hormonal boxing ring
her radical hysterectomy and bipolar disease
my teenage hormones and bipolar disease
words were lost down sieves and drains
sewage
rats

her emotions were like a box of steel
mine, darted off walls
storming
explosive
unpredictable

words were in the
cookie dough

in the oven
they screamed and screamed
until they were cooked and eaten

camp of Roch

my father
went
to a
private school
Sir Joseph Williamson's
in Rochester, Kent
camp of Roch
surrounded
by a Roman wall
built 55 B.C.

he did not
regret
not becoming an engineer
a teacher
a veterinarian

his sense
of adventure
wrote exam
for P&O
Peninsular and Oriental
Steam Navigation Company
passed exam
but eyesight failed him
excellent eyesight
required of cadets

instead apprenticed
as a machine mechanic
with his uncle
he traveled
round the
British Isles
on his motorcycle
to naval

and air force centres
doing stock control
for parts

Auntie Eileen
worked at
Avro Rose Aircraft
which made
bombers
during the war

he moved around
he moved around
and then he met
my mother

the child

fighting hard for my homeland
my territory of self
impositions, rigid religious
values – the child
unknowing
struggles to survive

blindness, rigidity
dominance of a wishful self
practicing warfare
on the small
undeveloped
territory of child

the child
a fertile field
a deep still pond
a silver star, sparkling
dazzling our
gaze

the parade

in a plain brown box
an old picture box
I selected one
not from memory
a black and white picture
this happens
all the time
picture leading memory

Polly, Eileen, me and others
there we were
wheeling our doll carriages
in the parade
down Cedar Terrace
dressed in our mothers' flowered dresses
wearing hats with veils and flowers pinned on
wobbling on high-heeled shoes

a sunny day
bright, clear, blue
no wind
only the song of a bird
giggling young girls
carriages, dolls
hearts beating
in anticipation
of winning
first prize
in the doll carriage parade

a little surprise was in store
a sweet dear little thing to behold
dressed up in a white frilly frock
my little doll had grey fur
green eyes with a glint
lay with paws and legs in the air
if my memory is accurate
first prize first prize
meow meow

Mrs. Bacon's steps

Middleton, England, aged 7

there is
a picture
of me
sitting
on Mrs. Bacon's
steps
with her dog

I had
a little
brown tweed
jacket on
and short-cropped
brown hair

time travel
1957
spoiled and
slightly hysterical
young girl
a bit
of a thief
uncontrollable

already
showing signs
of emotional
disturbance
bipolar
in today's
terms

everybody
clattering
their tongues
like
knives and forks
couldn't get
the young girl
to bed

crying
upset
alone

crying
upset
alone

have
been
that way
ever since

Teddy touches me

the teddies' names
were
Peter
Rupert
and George
George had no ears

worn out
hugged to death

my mother
never
touched me

instead, she
told me
when and how
to do things
contained me
in a box

once I said
"you do not
love me"
surprised, she was
taken back

unimaginable
for she
had served
this family
with such
diligence

tantrums

almost as if
in slow motion
the jelly broke,
glass, colours
flying

emotions, whirling
out of control
again
unable to resolve
conflicts
with no centre

put a net
around the child
pour cold water
on her
what will
the neighbours think

she curls up
on her cushion
with her cats
purring
in her ear

broken pieces of glass
or, my personality

there is not really much
but broken
pieces of glass

rotating
like a wind chime
inside my body

a mixed media
of feelings
perceptions
thoughts

the glass ball
on the Christmas tree
has been broken

the kitten
cuts her feet
briefly light
reflects
on the broken pieces
before it is swept
up

down, down

down, down
down
in the valley
so low
so low
so low

dark thoughts
waters deep
a child
on the edge
falling into
a deep, dark
hole

mommy
hold me
touch me

Presentation

mother and child

her skin
is radiant
she glows
blue
pearl white
in the dark
like a
firefly
a candle
a star

her body
is a
sacred vessel
to carry
the new
miracle
of life
changing
beyond
recognition
a love hate
relationship

feelings
sprout
reaching
stretching
vines
on the
garden wall
peonies
pushing
through
the soil

mother
the mother
give her
a blue velvet
cushion
to lay
her head on
wash
and perfume
her feet

celebrate
with her
the age old
story
of the universe
unfolding

an egg

my son
used
to say
he was
hatched
out of
an egg

I am
beginning
to think
I was too

I have
no
mother
I have
no father
I have
no history

surreal
maybe
I was
dropped
out
of a
flying
saucer
or down
the
chimney
by a
stork

I find
myself
in someone's
kitchen
being
called
a strange
name
mother

ground glass

life was
a living hell
digesting
ground glass

one minute fine
the next
without warning
withdrawal, distancing
total 'capsulization'
white light

I raged against
imagined attackers
from the past
tore my nightie
to shreds
while wearing it
ran
into the snow
barefoot
staring at the moon

curled up
in a fetal position
moaning
like a
lost child
hoping
the enemy within
would subside

humane but not ethical

I was never a good mother
I gated the environment
no sleep left me penetrable
the decks swirled like a drunken sailor
fearful that my young sons would get hurt

the street was a barrier
cars whizzing by on either side
sometimes I would bang on the hood of a car
if it infringed on the pedestrian walkway

the world was a threat
sound and motion
a world without trust
a surface to hold me up
a sky that suffocates

with scientific expanded knowledge
they should be able
to thumbprint a bipolar woman
then she could willingly be sterilized
putting an end to
traumatized children
in a raucous family
emotions erupting from embers
humane but not ethical

love of old things

rug frayed
at the edges
grease spots
on the walls
pictures painted
long ago
yellow and cracked
bent forks

the bed
sags in the middle
a stain
here and there

my life
is a river
flowing in my veins
devastation, fear
of a flood
drowning
in your own blood

turkey

as Christmas draws near
my feathers
are being plucked
one by one

sleeplessness beckons
exhaustion

not only
do I look foolish
but I have
a fear and dread
of what's to come

a bloodbath
a beheading
feet severed
a torso
sort of thing
left
for the beloved
Christmas feast

the necklace

around my neck
hangs
a silver necklace
reminding me of
who I am

moon and stars
reflect
my necklace
cool and glittering
sparkles, ice

my necklace is
mobile,
tight
to the point
of strangulation
it has me
gasping for air

long, reaching
into the
depths of the earth,
it travels
down rivulets
into crystalline caves

my necklace
reminds me
of who I am

the censor

deep in the pit
of my stomach
in the well
of my being
there is a censor
who will
not let me do
what I can do

my body
registers
his will

words
cannot
get out
they march
back in
blocking
my breath

the throat
is tight
a fleshy
underground
tunnel
leading me
to my divided self
the past

the no-good mother 1

Budd
it is
almost
as though
you
are not
here

students
share
their poetry
a flow
electrical
logical
piecing
together
a larger
statement
of what
lies
beneath
the screens

those
darn mothers
still
hold a
primordial
place
in our ideologies

but in
my mind
I am
a no-good mother
my feelings

have been
sucked
out of me

my children
are products
of American
advertising
demanding
plugged in
I don't know
if I can
salvage them

one word
that
does
give me
a great
deal
of pleasure
mother fucker
mother fucker

the howling

the howling
strikes terror
in me

a meeting of the local coven
alcoholic, close-knit
a mosaic of broken lives
creative,
beyond belief
exclusively themselves

I am not a part of this

Dear Juliet
pardon
my absence

the witch

my mother
was a witch
I am
one too
no teeth
a crooked finger
pointing at children

my mother's arrows
were sharp
I split off
hiding
under blankets
in corners
dressing up
in disguises

my mother is dead
but she lives in me

I wear a black cloak
and tell my children
what to do

they
do not
listen

the S-word

suicide
a crisis state of affairs
the will refuses to continue
to find meaning
in the trivial constructions
of a day

some lives
are not worth living
no crystal chandeliers
to light the way
no paths
through the forest
that lead to a palace
filled with the riches
accumulated
during your story

it is not
the girl crying wolf
rather an excruciatingly
lonely space
a desert of boredom
where shadows are larger than light

my ineffectiveness with my
children is outlined
it has to be pointed out to me
that my beloved cats
do not distinguish
bipolar and borderline personality disorder

secret monsters

when I am dog tired
deep down below
an ambiguous voice
declares itself

blasphemous language
often, with a highly sexual content
pokes out its unseemly head
to scream and thrash about

language from a deep abyss
dirty tributaries
foul-mouthed monsters
who live in my
subterranean landscapes

loud mouthed
the desire to smash and hurt
to feed the monster within
to let out a little vengeful steam
is the only way to calm the beast

in some ways
I live a life of pretence
hidden
shameful
feeding the snake within
with disgusting morsels

quicksand

a life and death
struggle
suffocating
in a cylinder
stuck
between stations
underground

darkness, panic
tight in the throat
spastic, narrow
air cut off

the words
cannot
get out
they march
back in
clogged
a sink
a garbage dump
quicksand

throw me
a branch
quick

Altered States

the cat queen

brown wooden bucket
a rope
falling
down, down, down
the stone well
water, still
dark and deep

ah, a door
little brass handle
my hand turns
ah, a crystal room
reflecting light
through
a rainbow prism

there on a
purple velvet throne
with gold trim
she sits
the queen
silver and white robes
blond hair cascading
to her waist

but wait
strange demonic eyes
green with slits
there reigns
the cat queen

a small child
kneels and begs
for permission
to leave

ding, dong, dell
pussy in the well

a land with no weapons

traveling from the class
down the stairs
to the outside
a hedge —
dialogue, how to
get through it
horns of a dilemma
conflict, debate

breaking through the hedge
hurt a living plant
climbing over, hurt
a living plant
the hedge becomes momentous
the rest of my life in
the shelter of this hedge, dialoguing
how to get through

in a flash
a wheelbarrow found
the hedge is six feet
I am five feet two

landing on my back
everything was green
but frustration grew
weapons undefined
desire to run
through the streets in the dark

my worst fear is men
they are a weapon
they plunder and terrorize
a primitive ripple of fear
it conquers the territory
of self, of child, of woman
for only their satisfaction

primitive times re-visited
naked bodies
wrestling
my body is enweaponed

eagle

perched on a branch
gliding
a miracle of flight

altered state
my arms outstretched
look I am
an angel

I feel
the white feathers
I learn
the art of flying

the air is
cool and blue

my body is
weightless

we speak without
words
for we have
no tongues

we touch
without hands
for we
have no hands

we share
a communion
telling of
the many wonders
of the world

the bodhisattva

she wanders through the streets
a heart as big
as the whole outdoors
warding off criticisms
from voices long
ago dead

how do you
lose
rolling the dice of
compassion?
the fashion in the 90s
: to give
politically/correctly

the knife of deconstruction
blasts
beliefs, values, ideals
the high-rise
terminology
-laden
hierarchical
transcendent, dualistic
world
crumbles (post
-modernized)
leaving us with
No Thing, powering our appetites
to violent
pornographies

karma
equals Choice
equals Action
equals Identity

where does this yearning
come from? the bodhisattva's loving
compassion, undifferentiated
interconnective, doing
and undoing

do we have any
other choice?
in our best dress
our Sunday best
our best frame of mind
— compassionate be

I exist between myself
and you

transparent wings

I am a moving target
transparent wings
veined with jewels
flapping in distraction
flitting from flower to flower

hidden agendas
thoughts cemented
aimed, ready to go
destination, direction
aim, fire

Cornered. Torn wings
pinned to the wall
one small drop of blood
staining
the jewelled net

fear of going manic

I am
beginning
to lose
things
in black holes

my wallet
my glasses
knife and fork

I am
sliding
in and out
of a hole

thoughts end
abruptly
never
to be
completed

the inner terrain
becomes hilly
I am on a
tilt-a-whirl
at the fair

the crack
in the door
has meaning
the ants
in the bathroom
are starting
to alarm me

head spinning

head spinning
ideas bouncing off the wall
a free
for all

surfing the waves
running like a mustang
on the beach

plunging
diving into a deep, dark pond
heartbeat
excitement

incestuous ideas
tangled like vines

a ladder
placed against
the wall
aerial view
farther and farther away
spinning off

natural and man-made consequences

definition, Webster's New Collegiate Dictionary
consequences, n.
something produced by a cause or necessary
following from a set of conditions
— where you sleep?

importance with respect to power to produce an effect
— who has the power?
— who doesn't have the power, maybe
the youngest child?

moment, social importance
the appearance of importance
self-importance

as a result, consequently

deduction, or
walking around a mountain trail
following as a result
or effect

not only, then

removal of the trees and then exposure
to the sun, rain and wind …
may cause degradation of the soil

observing logical sequence
looking at language which follows
or, as Margaret says, communication exists
between people, or
the postmodern term, truth
exists in discourse between people
not right or wrong
either/or dichotomy, bad or good

truth is a long winding sentence

do not go gentle into that dark night
fight, fight against the dying of the light

a faded memory
bright sunlight disinfects
hang your underwear on the line
the light is too bright, Orion
I cannot see
(I have always been a light-sensitive person, especially in the
morning. Even Nature bids us welcome with dawn.)

Margaret's Wheel
(from Sherod Miller, Couple Communication Program)
entry point, sensing
I see ...
I hear ...
I smell ...
BODILY FUNCTIONS
it all depends on the entry point
where you GO next
(for me it was the senses)
I see a bright light
I hear the flapping of wings
I smell bodily functions

bodily functions
my entry point is the senses
then I feel
LOUSY
my breath smells
curiosity killed the cat

Uncle Joe's Mint Balls
Pure Cane Sugar
no artificial additives
oil of peppermint, Great Britain
waving flags, the red banner

menstruating women should not enter the sacred ground
cross as a symbol of suffering & affliction
cross as an excuse
cross over the bridge and see what's on the other side
(Little Flower) (Bear) (Monkey) (Pussy)
(Kitten) (Girl) (Darling) (Bonnie Wee Pet Lamb)
ingredients:
pure cane sugar
oil of peppermint
cream of tartar
best if used by 8 Aug 98

you're my peri weri winkle
my jelly and my jam
my fairy, my canary
my bonnie wee pet lamb
you're my great big bunch of sorrows
my laughing cockatoo
and here is Mary Cockaband
it's cock a doodle doo!

The black bird leads me into a forest. It is commonly thought
that black is an evil colour but I have discovered otherwise.
This is one of the advantages of living in Toronto – one of
the most multicultural cities in the world. There are many
languages but only one which is spoken and understood and that
is English. English has uprooted other languages. It is the
language of dominance. The trees no longer have roots to
reach out and suckle mineral water from the delicately veined
underground tributaries. And this is why we call the earth,
mother. Maybe this explains why women have osteoporosis.
The chemical wash has ceased to lubricate the bones from
whence comes the seed of life. Although I must admit it
doesn't taste very good.

Stick it in and let her bleed.
I am weak. Blood is flowing from between my legs in an open
torrent.
My blood pressure's down.
I am weak.

It takes everything in me to get through a paragraph. It takes all the blood in me to get through the English language, starting from the first drop of blood which stained Indra's jewelled net – reflecting like mirrors –

stars
moons
and the cosmic universe
in my cloak
I am a princess
dancing through a field
of irises
I always knew artists could see clearly. What I didn't know
is that a woman can write clearly despite her
origins
in the bone of man
commonly known as a bone-on
erection
reaching up to heaven
and he rose up
his whole body
towards heaven
penetrating the sweet sticky
cotton candy
(a bit like
Walt Disney)
the strands
get
stuck in your teeth
and make your breath
stink.
And then have one of
          Uncle Joe's
                    Pure   Good
                         Mint Balls
                    Reg'd Trade Mark   No. 538700
                    e 191.4 g   200 g. inc. wraps
          Made By Wm. Santus & Co. Ltd.
          Wigan, England

the light was bright
a stone was thrown into a deep pool
like a thought
connecting
slowly
drawing circles
on the surface
of the water

I dive into the deep, cool water
I am wearing
a big organ of
skin –
cold, wet, odourless
a bit like death
I stand on a rock
my hands reach up
to the sky
I bend over
orifice delight
a gendenic interracial
chocolate bar
I feel connected
at last
now I know
why I hated
to see
babies bayoneted
on television
the cold dark spear
metal
man-made
in England

don't worry
it will get lighter
a large blue candle
hand-made, all natural
to pull me down
the long dark tunnel
but I can't breathe
there is something stuck

in my throat
a wishbone
has caught in my throat
ripping the lining
bleeding to death
all alone
in the vaginal desert
dry, brittle
disregarded
afraid of falling
afraid of crawling on your stomach
chronic indigestion
he can't eat fried foods
it upsets his stomach, dear
the ebb and flow
of pussy – oh – oh – oh
pussy

"Why does she have so many cats, mother?
"You don't like cats because they smell and scratch the
furniture
"Have you ever looked
into a cat's eye? I feel
terrified
cold
my arms are up
over my head
pinned down
by your knees
"But mummy, I don't like lumpy mashed potatoes. There's
lumps in it. I find it hard to swallow."

this picture
always terrified me
coming up for air
diving deep into
the dark cold pond
But mummy: "There's something down there!
It's creepy and crawly."
Well, let me ask you this:
"What are little boys made of?"

Snakes and Snails
and Puppy-dogs' tails
"And darling, what are little girls made of?"
Sugar and spice
and everything nice.
I understand
I see
the veil has been lifted
the light doesn't
seem so bright
I can see a little better
I know why I didn't like
the show
        Margaret's Museum
body parts in bottles
preservation
women's work
preserving male parts
in memories
perhaps you can start all over again
rinse it off
boil it down to get rid of the salt
salt retains water
I don't believe it
salt makes you fat
and not the healthy kind, dear
you smelly old bag
she's nothing but an old bag
"You know how many cats she lives with
"Thirteen.
"And they sleep on her clothes."
The other day I saw a funny
looking lady hobbling down the stairs in
black leather
high heeled
laced up boots
she had three bags
that were so heavy
she could
barely
lift them

Baa! Baa! Black sheep
Have you any wool?
Yes, sir. Yes, sir.
Three bags full;

One for the master
One for my dame
And one for the little boy
Who lives down the lane

at the bottom
of the deep dark hole

I'm terrified
be careful
you don't fall in
the surface is rough
like that picture in
your office
the seascape that I noticed
where the little boat
is going
up and down
up and down
up and down

swallowed up
swallowed up
swallowed up

please don't throw up here, dear
in the bag
    the bag
    the bag

"Oh, look, mummy, she's a bag lady!
She's wearing all that
jewellry
Honey, some people think

certain stones
can ward off bad smells
and insects.
You know.
Like mummy puts in
the clothes to keep away the moths.
I don't want any holes in
my clothes, mummy.
As long as you're clean
and you don't have
any holes in your underwear.
But mummy
my underwear smells
there is a yellowish, sticky
stuff running out of my
body

I need to dive into a deep
dark pool
where there is no current

Will I come up smelling
of irises or daisies?
The first flower of spring
mother earth, frozen & cracked
I can see it now
dancing around the meadow
with your friends
I can see you
you're in a circle
a circle
a circle
mummy
the stone has fallen into the
water and it is making circles
that connect with each other

and then it all

disappears

2　The Bodhisattva

Although the wind
blows terribly here,
the moonlight also leaks
between the roof planks
of this ruined house.

– Izumi Shikibu

Asylum

ambulance

communication
farewell family
loving me
as I am

quarrelsome conflict
I thought I would die
fading, fading
finding me there

the children
a sick child for a mother
love is
all there is

I have come to drink at the high altar of intelligence

I have come to drink at the high altar of intelligence.
i.e., The Grey Cement of Psychiatry.
There he goes Dr. Grey Tweed Jacket.
Tall, Affected, Razor sharp assessment.
A traffic cop of conversation.
I am not a PERSON.
Only a source of Information.
His office is like a white CELL.
No divergence or distraction.
Only a small pottery vase to express his humanity.

after talking to Dr. G

holding an icepick
hearing it
chip away at my spirit
disarmed

the knife

shining
in the sun
I noticed
a knife
in the ashen
volcanic landscape

I am a
volcano
my red hot
burning centre
threatens to
spew out
without warning
a knife
a hatchet

I am
a young woman
on a mountain top
I notice
a knife
in the ashen
volcanic landscape

hidden
29 years
running for my life
torn black stockings
gravel beneath my feet
black out
black out

memory gaps
can we ever
tell the truth

the gravel pit
three low life men
driving, driving
back back to town

my mind racing
strategizing
escape, escape

a gas station
a place to pee
get out
make a call
the car screeches away
I copy the license number

memory gap, memory gap
walking up
walking up the stairs
to my apartment
in terror
being followed
the paranoia
sets in

the intellectualization
of a crime

a rainy Sunday

a rainy Sunday
another hospital
10th Floor South
Psychiatric ward

bitterly cold, damp marrow-piercing rain
a stay-in, reading, writing, chatting, phoning, kinda day
anodyne
sleeping pill wonder
non-addictive
no side effects
no harm done
can't complain about that, doc

a community
a collage of stories
physical, emotional, sexual abuses
traumatized
chemical imbalances
genetic inheritances
caused or contributed by
wishbones in the throat
on festive occasions
birth during tornadoes
sandstorms, tidal waves, floods
and other natural or unnatural disasters

in England
country of my birth
no central heating
woollen vests and underwear
sitting around the fire
the custom
hot water bottles or heated bricks
tea, tea and more tea

a dream

lights on, stories being told
men hustling in the halls
and what do I do
start washing
my dirty underwear

the realm of belief

a strip of lights
horizontal, vertical
coming and going
in and out of no where

five in the morning
illicit relationships, drug deals
manics, who can't sleep
like me
monks praying for light

the lonely night people
homeless, even with beds
no one to talk to
wandering the night landscapes
inner terrain

no wonder people
believe in god
listening in silence
up there
in the cosmic universe

washroom

washrooms
downstairs, a long corridor
put fear and dread
in me

remembering
the loss of innocence
first sexual experience
rape gang

broken trust and faith
psychiatric ward
15 year old girl
falls into a dark hole

48 this month
today
Friday the 13th, 1998

diagnostic roulette

personality disorder
depression
post-traumatic stress disorder
bipolar disease
putting labels
on my pain

a shot
in the dark
ready, aim, fire

labeling, re-labeling
tearing holes
in my shoddy identity
patching it up
uneven thread

the parts
spinning around
a kaleidoscope
of self
bits of glass
glistening in the sunshine

just don't walk on it

Gerstein Centre

Spiritual Oasis, Isolation Ward
a warm friendly house
clean and orderly

I saw
anorexia
a statement of revolt
schizophrenia
a tight-mouthed stare
ritualistic protective behavior
necklaced to the point of strangulation
depression
lying around stretched out
suicide attempts
the day after
no bars and barriers

a lot of lonely people
holding a small candle
on their journeys

I reach out
to one little black girl
young and bright
a symbol of our future
God help us

Thank you
I am still human

sweet young thing

sweet young thing
little black bird.
forgets to eat.
one hand could
crush her little bone
and did

I am the universal child

I am the universal child
true and innocent
this broken doll-child
flirts with a dark side
chanting schizoid phrases
choosing a madness over pain
vaporizing and slashing the air with knives
unbounded anger
dissipates a broken world
which could have been
otherwise

the psychiatrist

you keep me straight
you keep me sound
isn't that why
we keep the psychiatrist around

you are a miner of
the human psyche
digging out precious rivulets
diamond, gold and silver

where is my ego in all this
you guide, sort and puzzle
that is what you are good at

but I am still
a tent without a pole
a treasure box without a key
a person without a centre

does this disease always
keep me dependent
on the skill of the psychiatrist

rendering me a stray cat
a man injured in battle
an orphaned child

a lifelong struggle

initial disclosure – dumping the self

no limits
crude constructions
of my history
of myself

painting
the past
in
black and white
like an
old picture
stashed
in the bottom
of my closet

vomiting
up the past
cleaning up
the mess
opening
the windows

embarrassment
feelings
the personal
all too personal

feelings

swept under a rug
worn as undergarments
next to the skin
I keep
a part of myself
hidden

in the quicksand
of my soul
these feelings
lay like objects
a knife
a hatchet

I am a
volcano
red hot liquid
burns my
inner psyche
swirling, whirling

making me
unpredictable
a threat
a potential monster

inside out
outside in
the feelings have become
statues in the garden
monuments to a crime

a carpet of wet leaves

blood on the ceiling
blood on the floor
blood on the bed sheets
blood on me
blood on me
blood on me

Transference

a patient's love song

full lips, intelligent
slow and deliberate
the way you say
your name
Pallavaraiyan

my body is warm
you slip in and out
of my mind
I have found you
at the end
of a long
journey

I love you because
you are Indian
from another continent
a comrade spirit
a healer

the owl and the pussycat

the owl and the pussycat
went to sea
in a beautiful
pea green boat

you are the owl
I am the pussycat
you sit back, judge
and assess
I sit on my
velvet cushion

you have feathers
I have fur
I love you
even though
you are my
arch enemy

we are different
species
yet we share
a little boat

I can't hold your hand
we have no hands
I can't kiss your lips
we have no lips

we sit in our little boat
at the top of the world – waiting

there is a tunnel deep inside me

there is a tunnel deep inside me
connecting to the past
I walk, with a bundle in my arms, down the long dark corridor
when I let go of the parcel, I fall through the floor
and find myself in bed and bleeding
and sick of heart, never having decided anything
letting them decide for me
but it is me who has to live out the rest of my life
it is me who has to face my own death
my guardian angel will not be there to say,
"you did the right thing"
you were too young and immature to look after a baby
what could have been, isn't
the past is let go and the white handkerchief
flies into the air
the sea swallows up the last of my sorrow
I am left with a few wasted decades

the body as a temple for loving you

I will house you
in my body
waiting
without movement
for a miracle

I will press my lips
all over you
my tongue will enter
each orifice
whispering a
little song

I will imagine
we are on a small ship
dazzling, floating, lit up
lying on a feather bed

we look up at the dark sky
a star dangles
a little rope
to pull us up

a ball of wool

my mind can be like a ball of wool
tight, interlocking
sharp like barbwire
entangled

at other times, unraveling
a constructed protection
an enclosure
where thoughts romp around
like wild horses in a corral

my ball of wool goes with me

transforming, from place to place
loud, entertaining
a member of the circus troupe
then, sitting dumb in the corner
like a child who has been
unjustly scolded

the wool varies in colour
bright like the hues of a rainbow
then, without warning

grey
motionless
silent

possibility

my birthday, 49

I saw a volcanic mountain in the distance
spewing red hot volcanic
molten lava
a red hot tidal wave
grey, ashen
I lived in a hut on another mountain
I was safe and
I could watch what was happening

later
a week
a month
a year
a decade
I was walking on the ashen surface
and I saw two objects shining
in the sunlight
a hatchet
a knife
when he was alive my husband said
the fire was put out by means of the hatchet
being dumb, I didn't understand
I hacked him with the hatchet
and his
blood
blood
blood
put out the fire

melt down

for 30 years
my sexuality
has been frozen
in a gigantic
ice cube

entombed
glass-like walls
distancing me
my passions
solidified

no feeling
pulsation
in my robin's breast

"all the birds
in the air
were sobbing
and a-sighing
when they heard
of the death
of poor Cock Robin"

now,
in my 50th
year ...

my mind is a mattress

my mind is a mattress
lay down and relax
I will wash your feet
with my tongue
I will touch your
tired temples

let us wear white cotton,
for modesty,
and be lovers
in the mind

hold me tight
massage my thighs
let our feelings
fall like a carpet
of petals
from a
flowering
tree

infatuation

my heart
skipped a beat
when you said
I was infatuated
dare I put
a match
to the shaved
kindling

a warmth
radiated
from my heart
to the
picked flowers
of the meadows
long ago
when I was young
before I
fell into the hole

spring was
bursting out
my veins
sizzled
heart throbbed
for you dear
for you

food abuse

riding
the wave
of desire
breathe
through it

think of
apples
and ricotta
a small
saucer
with a
few raisins
and a
handful
of nuts
like
when I
was a
child
brought
to me
by
my father

the waves
ebb
and flow

food
was
the last
thing
on my
mind

life was
laid out
like
a shelf
full
of teddies
a grey
cat
called
Smokey
an
intimate
talk
with a
friend

darling

you are coming
in and out
of consciousness

when you enter
I smell
spring
magnolia blossoms
I hear
the pounding
of an
ocean surf

the warm
sunshine
of your glance
makes me
forget
I am
not here
forever

the coloured
leaves
are a
wet robe
for my body

the winter snows
sparkle
in the sunshine
of my love

darling
counsel me
look after me
love me

I will not
breathe
a word
of it

even to
the hummingbird
the little brown sparrow

you crashed

or, this is not a feel-good therapy

you crashed
down on me
broke my
fragile shell

a pathetic
little creature
emerged

I looked at you
and saw
a series
of metal sheets
folding over
your eyes

I lost my
power of speech
you became
a man of metal

I crawled
out of the office
on all fours
leaking a white
substance

straitjacket

Straitjacketed with mental illness
Medication is the only choice.
Trapped inside side effects
Memory and attention
Weighted down by fog.

What is it like to be normal?
No anxiety, depression
To have a realistic view of the world,
Without a cocktail of feelings and ideas,
Mixing up the puzzle of life –
Not knowing what is and what is not.

I am blinded by sand in the desert.
A tidal wave is seen approaching
(An old childhood nightmare revisits me.)
Floods cover houses to the rooftops.
Wind takes me up in the air,
Then dumps me down somewhere.

Insecurities unground my sense of self.

the owl on the branch

you sit there quiet and still
your notepad on your lap
lassoing my words and emotions
breaking down the wild horse
succumbing me to analysis and reflection

I look back
hoping to be in line
not speak too loud
or release your impatience or admonishment

yet, I come back week after week
even after you said I should
get a certificate for being normal
I don't even remember
wearing a badge of normalcy

shouting
broken thoughts like shattered glass
sketchy memories
a story with no beginning or end
the heart like an artery around the mind

on the outside of in
I stumble along from day to day
no clear definitions or goals
you are an outline
on the periphery of my vision
the captain of spaceship normal

it would be an accomplishment
to break free of this bond

a stream of words

a highway
starting at one point
destination unknown
an ex-plor-a-tion
of self
a sort of self
like fog rising
on the early morning
Atlantic coast
objects first unseen
slowly taking definition
jellyfish woman
no spine or will
a shell
without a creature

the ripples
in the sand
massage my feet
I leave
behind
this poem
for you

Stories

the circle

table of story tellers
pass the eagle's feather
or pick up an old blue bone
tell your story

counselors
hush
listen
do you have
a story to tell?
the human element
red trauma
reverberating around the world

lie in a forest
under ancient trees
soft moss for pillows
prick up your ears
a surround of
movement and song

the moon
the light
of the silvery moon
I tread
by a path on moonbeams
I wear
a silver necklace
to remind me of you

let the sun shine in

in the morning
I open
the shutters
the sunlight
floods in
healing
past wounds
light
to write
my morning pages

I marvel at
the wonders
of nature
the tree
painting intricate
patterns
for me
to meditate

the birds
arguing and chattering
planning their day

the sun shines in
the miracle
of morning light
after the
darkness
of the night

rooms

last night
I dreamt
I traveled
through
a tunnel
of rooms
connected
by doors
with
ornate handles
crystal
brass
carved wood

the room
contained
only silence
silence
a space
dark and quiet

listen, listen
people
are beginning
to tell their
stories

I am white

I am white
my students
are mainly
people of colour

they come
from places
like
the West Indies
Guyana
Ethiopia
Sri Lanka
Thailand
Afghanistan
and Canada

we share
our stories
to help
plough through
the hard ground
of learning,
SKILLS
denied
by reason of
an unjust system
poverty
opportunity
place
origin
race

I want
to learn
to read
and write

the magic
of a wand
the wand
is lifted
sparkles
stories
remembered
dreams
something new
discovered

silence fell
when Yuk Sing
said she hated
her mother and father
denied an
education
having
to work
at an
early age
her father
would break
a bamboo stick
in half
and beat her

time travels
Yuk Sing
lost her job
seamstress
at Holt Renfrew
communication skills
not adequate

I want
to learn
to read
and write

Rashidi shared
his story
the starting point
the Russian
invasion of
Afghanistan
he fled
Iran
Sri Lanka
illegal passport
to the U.S.
imprisonment

time travels
a father
with a wife
and three children
a long way from home
he cannot
bear
any harshness

I want
to learn
to read
and write

the stories
bring
us close
together
my heart
my heart

quilt by design
for 'Veronica II'

women's work
recycling memories
children's parties, Sunday best
stained sheets, a love nest

the garden
look at the garden

petals for memories

closer, closer
bend down, kneel down
smell the gentle roses
stitch them together
carefully, evenly

touch my pain
put the pieces together
know what best fits
my love for you

ah, Maggie

ah, Maggie, how could you do it
leaving behind
two beautiful young boys
your mother and an aunt
Sasha and Virginia
heartfelt friends and
me

you were a beautiful person
fine, intelligent, caring
a future, everything to live for
Maggie, how could you do it

what was your story?
untold and hidden
an adopted child of the world
your painful and unspeakable chains to addiction
lost, ongoing efforts to no avail

could you not have reached out your hand to me?
I would have stood by you
held your hand
wiped your tears
sheltered you from your fears

you are my lost daughter
a bond will live on
for you and all the lost daughters of the world
you are our loss
we will mourn you in a circle together

my soul sheds tears for you and your dear ones
my spirit rises, joining us as one
but Maggie, how could you have done it
we love you

my room

my room
is my home
I am
my room
everything
can be taken
from me
except
my room

brightly coloured
objects
in my room
my life is there
a window
looking out
on nature
contemplation
solitude

cats purring
warm soft music
the beauty of
an ancient vase
hiding
under a bed
covered with
plush maroon
I am hidden
no one
is there
the room
is dark
a large candle
lights my way

safety net

last night
on t.v.
I saw
a trapeze artist
perform
without a net

how deep
the negative
currents run
fear
anxiety
inner broadcast:
"you cannot do it"
you will be
exposed
lose
consciousness

I will find
a safety net
to take with me
wherever I go
a butterfly net
a fishing net
a tea strainer

my guardian angel

I am fond of my guardian angel
silver glistening spread wings
jewelled robes to befit a king
half man, half bird
you are there to protect me

he speaks without words
he comforts without touch
he is inside out and
outside in
a harmony of body and soul

when I am afraid
he is there
to look after me and
wraps me
under the blanket
of his wings

it is purple-dark there
his feathers are mauve-soft
a rainbow is melding
to form a safe place
for me to lie down

the miracle of perception

when I
look out
my window
I focus
on the
mise-en-scène
the miracle
of perception
framed by
my life's history
values
I have
struggled for
free flowing
feelings

my soul
selects
my image-story

today
it is
a little bird
with three-pronged feet
microcosmic dinosaur

on the
snowy roof
I decode patterns
while my cat
meditates
quivering, vocalizing
from his
territorial perch
the window sill

the donkey sanctuary

fondness for donkeys
the beast of burden
carrying supplies up mountains
for tourists and entrepreneurs
the humble beast who carried
Mary and her unborn child to Bethlehem
a symbol for a world on which to dwell

an Afghanistani terrorist
used a donkey
to blow up fifty people
my heart went out
to this defenseless beast
who deserved a better death than this
blown apart for the sake of human politics

poor little donkey, sweet little donkey
blood and dust, blown to smithereens

remembering a childhood rhyme,
my childhood imagination takes flight
"gently brays the donkey
at the break of dawn
hee-haw, hee-haw
hee-haw, hee-haw, hee-haw

poor little donkey, sweet little donkey
blood and dust, blown to smithereens

the past

the past
pulls me back
salt and water
blending
mixing
sun and rain
a rainbow
the dynamics
of a
present
thought
a rainbow
thought

the past
be careful
of the
undertow

the little
boat
sails
the red rivers
of blood
in the
veins
and
arteries

I am
my little boat
my little boat
is me

the pig's head on the table

the pig's head sat on a table
smiling, dripping with blood
I cried for its past
and it told me my future
little girl, you are going to be
a strong and proud warrior
you will acquire land and within
the roots of a dead spruce you will
find an ugly brown box
filled with treasure
go and fulfil your life
bountifully

the candle

the candle
elemental
burning low
power to create atmosphere
to let our memories out
of the memory box

a candle dims the day
barriers subside
starting point
the personal
an object in the past
imbued with meaning
telling stories of
life and death
love
marriage, broken marriages
children
winning and losing

time and place
the past
our stories
tell us
who we are

imagination
paves
a silver road
to the sun
telling us
who we could
become

3   Mother

The moon lays a hand on my forehead,
Blank-faced and mum as a nurse.

— Sylvia Plath

Memory is like the moon,
Which hath its new,
Its full, and its wane.

— Margaret Cavendish (1655)

Memory is the only
afterlife I can understand.

— Lisel Mueller

Memory

mist

mist
lifting off fields
the road
winds beside
the river

I put on
my binoculars
and focus
on my past

middle of the century
a Middleton, Manchester child
grandfather, Gerald Carroll
worked in a cotton factory
he sang at family gatherings
in a beautiful, Irish tenor voice

the mater, Ellen
was adored

immigration to Canada
in 1952
the family left behind
wept at the docks

grew up in Antigonish
Nova Scotia
scarred by religion
a trinity of traumas
the injustice of adolescence

where have I come from?
where am I now?
where am I going?

the brain: the back roads of my mind

I dream
of a road
where I grew up
Highland Drive
Antigonish
Nova Scotia

I was
driving a car
and saw
a small child
playing by deep water
could I save
the child?
would I save
the child?

in my dream
there is an
old lady
my mother is
my father
needy, dependent

this road
is superimposed
on other roads
with other stories

everything is
there
that was
in the back road
of my mind

the past is
the present
the present
flows through me

the trunk

my mind is a trunk
filled with long-forgotten
sensations
memories
stories

when I sleep too much
things surface out of time and place
mingling
these old tapestries
take on a life of their own
familiar, yet foreign

I become a time traveller
going back, not forward
to precious nothings
taking on a radiant meaningfulness

my home town
the river runs through Antigonish
large, old oak trees line the streets of Highland Drive
east, lies St. Francis Xavier University

mixed feelings emerge
hope for the future
shame in the past

the lid of the trunk closes

Pogo, Mrs. Tutty's dog
comforts me
sleeping at the bottom of the bed

glamour puss

in my mind's eye
I remember
an old photograph
dressed in a little brown tweed jacket
hair cropped short
looked like a forlorn orphan
where were the frills and curls
what was my mother doing to me?

maybe this was the seed
of my glamour puss ways
I have always adored purebred cats
Russian Blue
Siamese
Burmese-Chinchilla
Angora

beauty in stature
beauty in line
beauty in elegant poses

curled up and contented
claws knitting, stretching
sleeping with one eye open
respectful of their independence and privacy

the cat has encoded itself in me
posing for an audience
purring and grooming
dressing for the occasion
watchful, slinking around corners
to see what's on the other side

raindrops 1

raindrops
are not
always
innocent

drought
in Ontario
the Great Lakes
a 30-year
low

foods
in the prairies
everything
under water

I remember
thirty years ago
lying in bed

listening
to the rain
on a tin
roof
pounding
an avalanche
startling

worried
the baby
within
would
be wounded

memory gap

a hole in my sock
a ladder
in my stocking
I caught
my sweater
on a nail

my memory
stretches
to the country
back road

my stockings are torn
the rocks hurt my feet
a man is
chasing me
he said
he had
a knife
in his pocket
his pocket

I am
running, running
memory gap
back in the
gravel pit again
discussing
should we do it
again, again

ploughing the earth:
a process of poetic transcription

the process of uncovering
ploughing
digging deep
into fertile ground
the unexplored emotions
feeling the unfelt

memory scapes
the appreciations
of past landscapes
in the back roads
of my mind

a picture
of a lake
framed by the trees
a little man
I did not know
too well
contemplation
the beautiful lake
his retreat
from unending demands

light and shadow
stage their contrasts
telling their own stories
a natural paradise

the glass bottle

the old man
was
brought up on
stories
of sea going
vessels
a bucket and spade
sand castles
sailing ships

I remember
the poems
he read me
as a child
Robert Louis Stevenson's
A Child's Garden of Verses
the railway carriage
the land of counterpane
the moon

the toe walks
up the stairs
to bed

the faces
painted
on the
boiled egg

now he sits
and looks
at the ship
in the bottle
memories

little red motorcycle

when I
was a child
I remember
a little red metal
motorcycle

my father's passion
for motorcycles
was not a secret

brown leather jacket
rain jacket
and pants
goggles for
the wind and rain
can't you just see him
on his bike?

at seventeen
a Douglas
rode
five miles
to school
and back

then, while working
at Addressograph
a Velocette
slightly better
than before

the Scott
unusual
like a car
a little water-cooled
radiator
a better class
of bike

joined
a motorcycle club
trial runs
competition meetings
exploring
back country of
Lancashire
Yorkshire
North Wales
on little winding
country lanes

the B.S.A.
and sidecar
Birmingham Small Arms
made munitions and
rifles during the war

mum and baby
in side car
quest and
exploration
of the back
country roads

a freedom from
dependency
on bus
a cheap form
of mobility
travel and
fresh clean air

I close
my eyes
and can see
the trail
they have left
behind

sea captains, vaudeville, black and white film

conversation
a silver line
of memories
ships
theatres
film
dialogues
built on dialogues
his gift
of storytelling

my father's grandfather
Charles
lived in Bush Hill Park, Enfield
a sea captain
on the coastal sailing ships

my father
defends his sternness
it was
a hard life
at sea
in those days
but he never forgot
being held upside down
if he cried

for his father, Alphonso
crossing the Atlantic
was a habit
he traveled to western Canada
taking black and white film
but Canada was too vast

he packed up
and went
back to Kent, England
with his new wife,

Magdalena Loucks
a country girl
becoming manager
of a cinema

in those days
films were
a community affair
a stage show
in the evenings
little tables
meals and drinks
comedy and vaudeville

my father
related all this to me
in conversation
in living memory
over a glass of sherry

the button box

remembering that button
from your mauve coat, Mum
now it sits in a red tobacco can
with other old buttons
from sweaters brought by
your two sisters from England
forty years ago

mauve was your
favourite colour
with your steel-grey eyes
determined, dominant ideas
devout Catholicism
mauve was much gentler

now, mum
you are dead
we struggled
you and I
I wonder
if you were more
gentle
touched me
listened
when I was a child
would I be …

mother, other

mother, other
fruit of
thy womb
the struggle
goes on
after death

and I
never knew
you mother

I was sick
and you
were
sick

a mad fury
of claws and fur
my resistance
served
your dogmatism

I spent
25 years
saying no

you never
touched me
you stifled
my intellect

yet, when
you were
old
I was
a dutiful
daughter

it hurt
me
when
you said
you didn't
want to
die in
pain
but
you did

the dark angel

we are shadowed by contingency
the dark guardian angel
not knowing the time, the place, nor the day
where we fall on the road
not to be picked up

this fear permeates the day
opens up the seams
unbuttons our coats
whitens our skin
makes our eyes dull and vacant
we won't be seeing anything anymore
we are tucked in for a long, long night

what we haven't done
will not be done
this is regrettably sad
our curtain is finally drawn
our stories have been told
no more laughter
no more crying
perhaps, just a memory
in a friend or relative's mind

you don't have a body anymore
an intellect, a mind
you can't be mindful
seeing and hearing sweet things
you are only a memory in someone else's mind

no matter how healthy and accomplished
you will come to the end of the road
you can be artful but
you cannot trick the dark angel

the old daddy

sitting quietly
thumb circling
bright little brown eyes
looking out

gentle, ever so gentle
a true gentleman

forgetful, repetitive

putting aside
his motorcycle and sailboat
wanting to ride
the wild ponies

where do you go now
your memory
is gone

you sit
ever so quietly
ever so quietly

Healing

Bev's tent and the magical toolkit

I have decided
to give up
the cloak of
victimhood
and replace it
with a toolkit
which I sling
over my shoulder
wherever I go
whistling a happy tune

the bag
is bottomless
whatever I need
is there
I reach down
into it
   a flashlight
   a compass
   a map
magically takes form
providing me

deconstructing
reconstructing
transforming

in my travels
I decide
to visit
Bev's tent
at the bottom
of the deep
dark pit

I open
my toolkit
and pull out

a book
of poetry

we decide
to look around
for some twigs
to build a fire

we sit
and look at
the fire
sparking imaginings of
primitive times
feel the warmth
hear the crackle

the fire goes out
it is time
to fold up the tent
climb out
of the hole
with the help
of each other
and go home
home
home
home

the red cardinal

it is two in the morning
I cannot sleep
looking out the window
I see a tree
glistening with raindrops
decorating the sky with bare, brown branches
a Christmas tree!

gone are the French
white lilac blossoms
longed for and admired in spring
becoming a beautiful flowering bride
then slowly, the blossoms fall to the ground

winter is approaching
rain, ice, snow
unpredictable
damp, cold, alone

yet, the brown sparrows are fat
squirrels fight, screeching in the night
seeking out the last morsel of food
before winter sets in

yesterday, I saw a red cardinal
well fed, grooming its feathers
artistically contrasted to the
bleak surroundings
the sight etched in my mind

oh! red cardinal
a red lantern to light my way
along my path, in the darkness

Friday night

minus 24
another
Friday night
alone in bed
looking
out the window

the right side
of my window
is intricately etched
in frost
frozen rivulets
embedded
with stars
dazzling
from street lights

silvery white
on a canvas
of urban
night sky

I follow
the trail
of a plane
wondering
if I
will ever
be able
to fly

branches
stiff, white
pointing
their fingers
telling
me stories
without words

stories
without words

the necklace (2)

I am
my necklace
my necklace
is me

the circle
a full moon
pale gold
a silvery night

night stars
glitter
winter ice
an aura
of protection
a token
of my
truer self

the lace
is wound
around my neck
snowflakes fall
uniquely
brilliantly dancing
fairies skating
on a
moonlit night

the moon has a face

the moon has a face
like the clock in the hall

darkness, light
contrast
a deep dark pond
a beckoning night sky
undefined
a clear night
a full moon
a face
a crescent moon
hung around my neck
stars, supposed galaxies
look like twinkling diamonds
to me
standing
on the edge
of the world
looking at the night sky
wondering
where I have come from
where am I going

light
the sunrise of a new day
the memory of warm, summer sunshine
on my face
penetrating
my cool, dark soul

light defining
a flash
share understanding
light a candle
for me
for the little children
of the earth

spring

the buds
of the trees
looked very
rude
waiting
to burst

pushing
out of
the earth
red, erect
I was
delighted
to see
the peonies

the birth
of a baby
red and wet
not yet
beautiful

fresh, new
leaves
etch
the sky
like
the wallpaper
in a
Degas painting

a daredevil with a broken wing

I love to give to my son
he is the dearest, sweetest thing
a lone fawn at the edge of the forest
a baby owlet perched on a branch
looking into the dark night
a bear cub protected by its mother

he operates on a different plane
quiet, non-verbal
animals take to him
cats, dogs, even birds
he strokes Gracie's feathers
(his girlfriend's cockatiel)

he is a good son
respectful and obedient
despite his depressive-anxiety disability
with an alcoholic outlet to enable
he is starting to take responsibility for his own life
supported by CAMH, a psychiatrist and his GP

he doubts whether the new medication will be effective
I said it was with me
I can only tolerate one drink

intelligent and good looking,
unlike his mother
he has a lot of friends
a daredevil with a broken wing

I feel you beating

I feel you beating
in my veins
life force
the pulse of blood
in harmony as one

you have been my husband and friend
my teacher and philosopher

unfortunately, I have
slaughtered the lover in you
abused you erratically
sexually slandered
your body parts
when I am manically
on cloud attack
to ease the tight band
of tension and ferocity

I feel you beating
in my veins
life force
the pulse of blood
in harmony as one

listening, attentive
a true gentleman at service
big brown eyes
endearing, trusting and
golden

your Tiffany lamp

I left on
your Tiffany lamp
waiting for your return

sometimes I see you
slip around the corners
a flash here, a flash there

the light fills your room
casting its glow on your trophies and awards

many objects reflect you
the two pictures of Mahone Bay
your father's sign hangs there
G. W. Langen, Barrister-At-Law
promises unfulfilled

it is a little museum
telling stories of your travels to Nepal
a handmade wooden violin
a beautiful, colourful woven scarf

you are a real little collector
two masks from Colombia
various posters and a calendar from
the Woody Point Poetry Festival in Newfoundland

my special object is my father's
caramel-lacquered, Art Deco dressing table
my regret is that I didn't take my mother's

now, there is only solitude to befriend me
heart-throbbing silence to take my hand
the little spirits of fur animals to comfort me

full moon

on going to bed
I glanced out my window
and saw the full moon
looking back at me

what was he thinking?
was my day in a life worthwhile?
could he see what lay ahead?
pain, disease, the time of death

or was he just gazing in at me
to offer me moonlit comfort and support

I admired his gold-yellow sanded beauty
the wholeness of round
the halfness of half
the crescent hung on a gold chain
around my neck

moon in the sky
connect me to the universe

dark space
starlit nights

a full moon

mind over emotion

my mind
developing and getting stronger
feelings handicapped
(despite my fondness for them)
spinning, looping
taking flight
free, not reined
maybe even childish

people thought I was deep, interesting
a deep pond
a star in the sky
the sound of waves
crashing

the mosaic of emotions
can be a work of art
a heart breathing
pulsating with life
showers
on a tin roof
a strike of lightning
intuition

but it was my mind
that anchored me
in the storm
guiding, clarifying, working out
the puzzle
climbing the steep mountain

the mind, my friend

changing sky

I looked
up from
my book
downstairs
in the living room
through
the brown shutters

the sky
baby pink
and powder blue
the colours
teenage girls
like to wear

just
for a moment
then
a more
sombering scene
the sky
fluorescent grey

across the street
the old Victorian house
with its round
stained glass window
looking west

a bright yellow glow
a prayer

all of this
in the urban sky
at 7:30 a.m.
Sunday

the mermaid

half woman, half fish
glittering jewelled tail
worshipping
a naked woman's torso
still goes on

sailors, cruising
on their ships
beckoned by beautiful women
to the rocks

the sisters of the sea
weave magic nets
draped over fishing vessels

they sit on rocks
combing their knee-length hair
hiding their tails
beneath the surface

I am a bit like that

playing it safe

sometimes
on the streetcar
when the sun
is shining
I close
my eyes
and see pink

this is
an adventure
I enjoy

the chatter
around me
subsides
and I
am engulfed
in a
soft pink
blanket
peaceful enough
no feeling,
thoughts

just the reflection
of my eyelids
on my soul

cosmic crash

walking along Queen St. West
The Word on the Street
a young slim man
ran into me
cosmic crash

his hazel eyes
sparkled
in the bright sunshine
electric storm
young, clear
bright eyes

Home

the blue dragonfly
for Solveiga

you remind me
of a
blue dragonfly
a Zen garden
simplicity
stillness

the pond is
still and deep
the dragonflies
skim the surface
with precision
warlike sounds
showing off
their acrobatic
feats

you remind me
of a blue
dragonfly
blue, blue
quiet and deep
etched like
a Japanese painting

dragonfly, fly
soar
spread your wings
take flight

atmospheric love

high in the sky
above the clouds
bright and blue
I feel a limitless atmospheric love
high, bright, limitless

no boundaries, no critics
beyond words and definitions
only a total body feeling
of my love for you
a total feeling love

I am an angel of light
my own guardian angel
wings tucked in at the back
my nature and identity kept secret
secret angel of light

expanding and directionless
love like the air we breathe
outside in, inside out
a limitless atmospheric love
expanding, limitless love

come to me my imaginary lover
fill the crevices of my being
be my comforting friend
when I am alone and in need
come, fill, comfort

be my atmospheric lover
on earth and in space
I surrender myself to you

the sky
for Marsha

the sky is
smoky lavender
burnt pink
white glaze
and so are you

you inspire those colours in me

a thoughtful night
feet on burning sand
winter ice on a lake

you inspire those colours in me

lavender is lovely
pink is pretty
white is all

transformation

a bird's eye view
flight above normal
renewal, flux, reborn
on a higher level

stillness forms, then turbulence
chaos diminishing
hearing and vision, throwing and spinning me
round and round

I reach out to the sun
to quiet me in this chaos
holding on to a butterfly's wing
catching a ride on a bird's tail
soaring through the air
jumping across ponds
where golden fish and frogs dwell
flowering lily pads
float on the surface

I walk through the shady, thoughtful forest
contemplating and analyzing
my situation
nature soothes
allowing me respite

my metamorphosis

gold and silver

Roger is gold
his name means
good with a spear
he will fight injustice
wherever he finds it

I am silver
silver moonlight
silvery raindrops
on the window pane
a silver sheen
on a still, deep pond

complementary – gold and silver
solid intelligence, analysis, logic
contrasting dancing imagination
a twosome of 40 years
barely surmounting human difficulties

man woman
the sameness of same
the difference of different
understanding
same
different

gold intellect
silver imagination

love

love
a circle, no beginning, no end

the treasure chest of life accumulates

the button tin saved from my childhood home
the green button from Christine's Burberry
the mauve button from my mother's coat
each button had its own story and memory
yet they all got along in the tin

nature informs the city
the city sheds its light
etching on my mind

a landscape

the red rocking chair

I spend inordinate amounts
of time in this chair
watching movies
allowing the imaginative
landscape to arise
often accompanied by two cats
Jasmine and Blue George

it offers relief from
degenerative osteoarthritis of the knees
comfort
support
almost companionship

a red friend
we all three, gather
snuggle together
until relaxation, sometimes sleep
overtake us

this, chariot of fire
beckons me to old age
flying through space and time
gathering the dust of past
ancestors underneath
yet staying the course
determined to move forward

a medium from sleep to waking
providence
friendship
solace

the canoe

I am a canoe
a canoe is me
a small boat
floats
through
the forest landscape

knowing
trusting
the water
to hold me up

the canoe
me
the river
the trees
the sky
are one

all is one
one is all

mother

eternal mother
conniving tributary peace strategies
love and replenishment
look to the sun
the bare branches
outlining our destinies

reaching to the heavens
rooted in fertile ground
our arms reach upward
bare, rough and brown
the colour of the earth

take care, dear mother
look to the sunset
the glorious colours
I will be thinking of you

thank you

thank you

thank you   thank you

thank you   thank you   thank you

love

love   love

love   love   love

Veronica

Poem Notes

grey blanket, Gerstein Centre, feelings – These poems were previously published in *Resistance Poetry 2* (Hidden Brook Press, 2012).

rain on the tin roof – The 'Home of the Guardian Angel' – today the Chebucto Family Centre – was located in 1970 in the east wing of St. Joseph's Orphanage, Halifax. 'Dorothy and Gerard Murphy' would later found Murphy's on the Water, a restaurant on the Halifax pier.

the no-good mother 1 – 'Budd' is Budd Hall, Chair (in 1999) of the Department of Adult Education, OISE-UT. Responding to her poems written in course, he commented, "You speak for so many."

ground glass – The word *'capsulization'* is the first among several neologisms in the text. Others are: *enweaponed, gendenic, manics, scapes, halfness,* and *sombering.*

I have come to drink at the high altar of intelligence – In this and other poems, the names of medical institutions and individuals are changed, except where disclosure is permitted or innocuous.

the knife – This poem refers to an event in St. John's, Newfoundland, in about 1972. In a well-publicized trial, three men were convicted.

washroom – This poem refers to an event in Truro, Nova Scotia, in 1965.

Gerstein Centre – The Gerstein Centre, Toronto, was established in 1989 to provide "discharged mental patients" with short-term residential and crisis support.

quilt by design – 'Veronica II' refers to an admired substitute teacher about 1997-98.

ah, Maggie – 'Maggie,' imagined as an "adopted" daughter-in-law, died in 2015.

the pig's head on the table – This early poem was written about 1995.

Bev's tent and the magical toolkit – 'Bev' refers to a student colleague at OISE-UT.

the red cardinal – The 'window' in this and other poems in this part of the book is from a house on Sword Street in Cabbagetown, Toronto.

a daredevil with a broken wing – CAMH is the Centre for Addiction & Mental Health, Toronto.

your Tiffany lamp – The poet's husband was teaching in China (2014-16) when this poem was written.

the old daddy – This is the last of several poems on the poet's father, Gordon Eley. For his influence on his daughter, see Appendix.

the blue dragonfly – 'Solveiga' is Solveiga Miezitis, Professor of Adult Education, OISE-UT (2000), admired by the poet for her encouragement and teaching of 'personal values for transformation.'

the sky – 'Marsha' is Marsha McDonald, a close friend. The poem is the last written by the poet (in 2020) and is the only poem in the collection following her retirement to Nova Scotia in 2016.

Appendix

The following poem, written about 1953, is from the self-published booklet, *Random Thoughts*, by the poet's father, Gordon Eley. In its imaginative message of comfort to a young child can be seen constitutive elements in the poet's own imagination.

To a Tiny Tot Going to Sleep

Hark! What's that, a patter of feet,
Must be Teddy Bears in the street.
Listen! What's that squeaky noise?
Sure there's a wee mouse in the toys.

Pit-patter of rain on the window sill,
I believe the mouse is in the toy box still.
What's the streak of light across my bed?
Why that's only the moon, you sleepy head.

A rumble of drums and a ring of a bell,
Who that can be, I cannot tell.
A fairy light twinkles afar.
Could be an elf just lighting a star.

The howl of wind, sounds like the sea,
But I cannot sleep for the fear in me.
Put your head on your pillows, never fear,
Your dreams will be happy, cause Daddy's here.

Afterword

Trauma Poetics in *The Blue Dragonfly*

An inner impulse rent the veil
Of his old husk: from head to tail
Came out plates of sapphire mail.

— Alfred Lord Tennyson, The Dragonfly (1833)

It is in the nature of trauma to block its own story: the scorched-earth policy of a traumatic event burns even words. "Unspeakable," an indelible memory folds into amnesia, a *grey blanket*, the poet writes – *'the waves, the waves / are big, mommy / the cold, grey ocean / is deep.'* But the dark curtain of forgetting cannot hold. Unremembered and untreated, the anguished, melancholy spirit it conceals demands attention. It wants to be seen. And heard.

The Blue Dragonfly – healing through poetry is the story of one such event. Its unfolding is not merely a re-telling, but a series of re-enactments: a re-living of events, anxieties, and altered states; of relentless bipolar disturbance; of *memory loss – 'like / a stone / skipping backwards / over a pond'*; of breakdown, therapy, and recovery; and finally, of selfhood and memory regained, transcendence and forgiveness.

Poetry is first herald then divine to her illness. In the wake of a major breakdown, the traumatized poet finds herself at *'another hospital ... Psychiatry ward'* in company with other *'wishbones in the throat,'* as she writes in *a rainy Sunday*. Following a prolonged assessment, she is retained for outpatient therapy. A power for representing her chaotic inner world through creative language had been observed. Spurred by a voice from the past, she had started a diary shortly before. In the earlier notebooks, one can see the door to memory easing open. An inner landscape forms.

Journaling becomes increasingly poetic. Discrete feelings distil into discrete poems. Ultimately, they become a formulary or script for the relief of pain. Discovered by her psychiatrist, the poems would provide a cognitive breakthrough previously denied to the therapeutic discourse. The therapy would continue for 17 years.

Veronica Eley attended no workshops, never imagined herself a poet, is hesitant to think so even now. She wrote her "poetic diary" as a task assigned to her by psychological necessity. Having served their healing purpose, the poems were set aside, the journals put away. Even so, occasional readers recognized in the writing a severity for rendering a subjective experience (of trauma) representative and, as poetry, wholly visible. For this reason, gently encouraged, the poet permits her poignant and expressive story to be brought into the full light of day.

Two readers are imagined for this book: one sanative, the other literary. The former will have a sympathetic interest concerning the problems associated with healing trauma, and in particular, for seeing its enigmatic obscurity made transparent. The second, with stricter expectation, will look for poetry's exceptional authority to express human or spiritual extremes in a vivid, imaginative language.

The Poetic Manifest

The poems speak for themselves. Their selection and organization comes with the engagement and approval of the author. The 120 poems (of about 600 in total) are culled from diaries and notebooks and loose-leaf scraps. Most were written during two periods of activity, 1997-2002 and 2013-2015. The first of these gatherings pertains to the writer's initial breakdown and diagnosis, this period being by far the more productive.

The poems are arranged in a "thematic chronology," so that the progress from problem through process to resolution can be seen more clearly. In the actual process of writing, themes were continually being revisited: hope, terror, the fear of sinking or *'drowning / in your own blood'* (from *love of old things*), the pounding at the door of memory, the beauty and refuge of an alternative world. Such recurrences explain what may seem like occasional inconsistencies in style, especially in poems with longer and shorter lines. The variation indicates the evolution of the poet's style through diary writing. From a stream-of-consciousness prose, phrases begin to separate onto distinct lines. As feelings and thoughts atomize further, lines shorten. In the end, poems spill down the page like beanstalks or strips of recombinant DNA, with a clear structure, fruits of metaphor on the vine, and a secret story to tell.

Capitalized words, and the conventional use of punctuation, such as period and comma, infrequently appear. Commas preserve the readability or poetics of a line. Otherwise, prose markers identify moments of rupture: the shock of a sudden containment, the intrusion of authority. In the poem, *transparent wings*, lines flow poetically, until reined in by commas, then abruptly stopped, as the speaker finds herself, *'Cornered.'* Capital letter and period are signs that the speaker is experiencing a loss of self-autonomy, which then disrupts the poem. The self in these poems is preserved by attitudes in her voice: defiance in *I have come to drink at the altar of high intelligence*, resignation in *straitjacket*. In general, the poems in this part of the work reflect the distorting effects of an active disturbance.

It is worth taking a moment to comment on the most extreme example, *natural and man-made consequences*. This long, seemingly incoherent text emerges at the end of a series of poems showing a rapid mental decline. Despite its poetic shape, it is really a moment of disorientation (or poetic exhaustion) presented as a long internal conversation or dramatic monologue. The voice is deliberative and deranged, rambling around a single thread, rude and frank yet indirect. The poet signals her awareness of a disordered unity with the line, *'truth is a long winding sentence.'* The voice is her own, though others are present, including, notably, her mother, who speaks only here. The text itself is troubled, unpleasant, unpredictable, regressive. It is also intent on answers, as if the speaker is endeavouring to remove some unwanted substance from her mouth – perhaps the particle, 'man-' in 'man-made' – as she struggles, with distraction and faux patience, to confront a "monster." The speaker's mother is its surrogate. From 'rape gang' (in the poem *washroom*), a thread not made explicit in the poem winds through institutional actors – priest, policeman, and doctor – until cinched at the end by a precept of the Catholic catechism: better to die a martyr and save your virginity (like Maria Goretti) than submit and escape with your life. The event may be abhorred, but an imperfect victim is condemned. The taint of a wider complicity extends even to the solicitudes of institutional care. In *I am the universal child*, 'this broken doll-child' is treated not for an external injury, but for instability, for 'choosing a madness over pain.'

The traumatized subject is thus overwhelmed. Unable to name it, objectify it, or expel it, a golem of sorts lodges in her psyche, merging with her feelings, 'inside out, outside in.' The paralysis of her inner life is symbolized at the end of the poem, *feelings*, as the mute and menacing tokens of 'statues in the garden / monuments to a crime.' Moloch, as the monster may be called, is never required to speak. But in the disordered, traumatized text where "consequences" matter, he is for the first time challenged. Amid the scrum of wounded words, the reader is close enough to the source of the poet's originating trauma that we can sense its terrible reality, and how it looms over the "innocent" conversation between mother and child. Referring elsewhere to a second exposure event (in *the knife*), the poet asks, 'can we ever / tell the truth.'

The agonized linguistic moment of *natural and man-made consequences* is but the inevitable urtext of a trauma first speaking. Trauma authorizes the text – negatively, by silencing it. Words emerge as a form of resistance to it. This is the point of the incoherence in her first speaking. It is a struggle just to *find* words.

Which is perhaps why she starts with the dictionary, edging her way along the contours of Webster's definition of the word, "consequence," questioning its dry formulations, interposing the discontent (and insurgency) of her own mind. She is seeking *through language* a power of action, a vantage point from which to perceive and *oppose* the hostile stranger within. Inside the sanctuary of her journal, her voice becomes audible to herself, as she sounds the experiment with words. The words reply, fashioning for her a stance and, over time, a stylistic identity – a coat of arms, a shield, a lance – in what I call her *poetic manifest*. Metaphor is thus "selected" as her tool for combat, her weapon of insight. The protagonist now self-invented, the story can unfold. As told here, it is the story of a real-world survival, unconscious of archetypes and topics or literary convention, indifferent to affectation or romance. Trauma's authority ensures that the storyteller's voice, when it chooses to speak, will be authentic. The constraint is that trauma is so deeply in-woven – like a knotted mass in the brain, *'tangled like vines'* in a *'deep, dark pond'* (from *head spinning*) – that unraveling its *'tight, interlocking … barbwire'* (from *a ball of wool*) requires a patient, long, obsessive attention. Only then can the words and syntax be found to tell her story.

Poetry therefore gives necessary scope to the task at hand. The author cannot count on ordinary language. She distrusts, moreover, her native English on political grounds – for its "dominance" of other languages, whose roots *'can no longer … suckle mineral water from delicately veined underground tributaries.'* This kind of metaphorical rupture in her prose (in the urtext) is significant. It shows that language as *metaphor* is a medium on which she *can* rely. The notion of an "underground tributary" is one among several topographical motifs in the poetical language of the book. Light, water, and air, and their rough antipodes, darkness, blood, and ground, thus form part of a "natural" tool set for an effective poetic archaeology of the history of trauma. Light is a candle, crystal, sparkle, star; darkness, a pond or hole, a landscape, a cave; water is surf, rain, an underground tributary, blood in the vein. All serve as natural windows into the poet's inner world. As illustrated in the text, poet, subject matter, and metaphor are one. The glitter in *the necklace* she wears is a pathway *'down rivulets / into crystalline caves.'* When in the evolution of her story, metaphor finally takes to the "air," leaving dark landscapes (and the world of men) behind, she finds company with other comrades of the sky, dragonflies and hummingbirds, angels and eagles, sun, moon, and stars.

The Healing Narrative

The organizing principle behind the arrangement of poems in *The Blue Dragonfly* follows the storyline for healing: injury, treatment, recovery. Where the injury is trauma, the stage is set for a *psychological* drama. The overarching story is archetypal: from chaos to order, darkness to light. The poems – *'language from a deep abyss'* – are the candles lit by the protagonist to guide her through the catacombs, as it were, of an old house. It is a spiritual odyssey in three acts: first, the descent; then the intervention of a "miracle"; and finally, a journey of uplift and renewal. Following the Table of Contents, we comment briefly on the main section headings and on the episodes or "passages" each contains.

Part 1: Secret Monsters – This section covers the major part of the poet's life. As mentioned above, her task is to arrive at the moment of a trauma first speaking. Only then do the poems arise in real time, painting backwards, as it were, the scenes of her childhood, turbulent adulthood, and eventual breakdown. The constant looping and spiraling of images and motifs in the text is a reminder that trauma is a many-headed monster, like the Hydra that confronted Hercules, requiring constant decapitation.

Prelude – In the foyer of the dark house we are about to enter are five poems. They serve as an emblem for the reader. The first, *a child's tea party*, offers us the promising sign of the protagonist's fighting spirit, or instinct for survival, despite the snake that sits at the table. The poem also establishes a fundamental theme, invisibility – *'you know / that invisible feeling,'* the poet writes, *'lost and forgotten / before even conceived / and remembered.'* The formulation, "forgotten before even conceived," speaks to the sense of a profoundly "remembered" exclusion, felt not only as the "accident" of her personal birth, but as an intuition of homelessness or exile belonging to human consciousness itself. As hers is an allotment to trauma, this consciousness is retrospectively imagined as a darkness visible from within the womb. The succeeding three poems identify other, more specific themes: fear (of separation), a particular traumatic event (of four), and the central problem of memory loss. The Prelude concludes with a poem of prayer: *'saints and angels / protect me / from spilling / this cup of blood.'*

Childhood – The imprint and rudiments of the trouble to come are laid out. The poet laments *'warfare ... on the small / undeveloped / territory of child.'* This is the precipitating distress that undermines, predestines, and frames the life to come. The nine poems show us its complicated features: a bipolar inheritance, identified in the opening poem, *tortured words*; the ensuing power struggle, resisting control and *'rigid religious / values'* (from *the child*); and, critically, the loss of words, imagined as disappearing *'down sieves and drains'* or hidden in the cookie dough, where in the oven, *'they screamed and screamed / until they were cooked and eaten.'* The home is the scene, therefore, for a "developmental" trauma. From the brightness and promise shown in *the parade* to the poignancy of touch withheld in *Teddy touches me,* the poems in this section speak variously to her sense of shattered self and brave use of small resources.

Yet as the remaining poetry in the text makes clear, the story itself is a complex and layered affair. The parental divide – discipline and control on the one hand, solace and indulgence on the other – is but one factor in the formation of her personality. Historical and social circumstance, other family dynamics, and in particular, the intergenerational aspect of mental illness – all play a role. In the end, mother will be forgiven. But in the deeper underground is the sense already in childhood of a vulnerability exclusively the poet's own, of a destiny to "neurosis" which future traumatic experience and multiple diagnoses, respectively, will exacerbate and confirm. It is not surprising, then, that her childhood is marked in these poems by a roiling personal volatility. In the penultimate poem, she imagines her personality as like *'broken pieces of glass / rotating / like a wind chime / inside my body.'* The final poem, *down, down*, is a plaintive yielding to the pathos of despair.

Presentation – In this series of poems, a 30-year period of untreated mental illness presents itself in different guises. Trauma is now in the ascendant. The principal theme is the poet's acknowledgment of her alienated motherhood. In *an egg*, she finds herself being called *'a strange / name / mother.'* Life was a *'living hell,'* she says, daily *'digesting ground glass.'* She feels ineffectual, ambivalent, paralyzed, enraged. Identifying her bipolar disease in *humane but not ethical*, she is *'fearful that my young sons would get hurt.'* We note the words, "ethical" and "fearful." They are evidence, equally, of a felt responsibility to motherhood and of a countervailing force that would disable and attack it. She imagines this force as the dark, "other" side of herself, not yet recognizing that it is the traumatic wound speaking through her. Self-reproach, humiliation, shame, resignation, are plagues of feeling that nonetheless suggest that a struggle is taking place, that a discourse or "awakening" is in progress between herself and her "other." She cannot yet articulate it, but the poems show – as written after the fact – a growing awareness of the *'monster within.'*

The wind that blows through her, in fits of mourning and rage, resonates with the "voices" of past loss – of her daughter, her mother's affection, of her mother's own lost story – and of shame, for repeating in herself the entangled relation of victim and perpetrator. And while shouting and violence is not precisely speech, the *activity of struggle* in the "dialogue" between herself and her dark other indicates that a hard reckoning, or "articulation," is at hand. In the Christmas poem, *turkey*, she expresses *'a fear and dread / of what's to come,'* of *'a bloodbath / a beheading.'* The impulse to violence – to self, to others – is palpable also in poems like *the no-good mother 1*, *the S-word*, and *secret monsters*. In the last, she identifies *'an ambiguous voice'* from *'deep down below,'* *'foul-mouthed monsters'* who – when she is *'dog tired'* – *'scream and thrash about,'* feeding a *'desire to smash and hurt'* so that they themselves may be fed.

Her task, then, is to find words that will speak for *her*, not *it*. In the absence of a language adequate to confront the monster – by "seeing" and revealing it – she remains vulnerable to her original harm. The blockage of words is therefore an important motif in this "episode" of poetry. In *the necklace*, she is *'gasping for air.'* In *the censor*, *'words / cannot / get out / they march / back in / blocking my breath.'* The choppy lines, the faltering words, convey the sense of the poet's speech as clogged in a *'fleshy / underground / tunnel,'* a tunnel, she says, that leads *'to my divided self / the past.'* This same sensation of *'darkness, panic … air cut off'* is repeated in the final poem *quicksand*, when the ground beneath her finally gives way.

Altered States – The inevitable collapse occurs, as the protagonist's exhausted psyche turns hallucinatory and euphoric. The poems here are characterized by extremes of feeling and varieties of "imagined" motion, from the sense of limitless flight to the anxieties associated with 'spinning,' 'running,' 'plunging,' or 'falling.' Dreams, imaginings, and visions (*Prozac*-induced) present the shifting facades of a delusion of flight. The poet finds the correct metaphor for this in the idea of a *'tilt-a-whirl / at the fair'* (in *fear of going manic*), where she is *'sliding / in and out / of a hole.'* In other words, she is repetitively experiencing the one, single motion of a *fall*, except in this moment she is at the site of her trauma, the "hole," above deep water. These various elements are already apparent in the opening poem, *the cat queen*. Here she imagines her fall as controlled, as she uses a rope to descend into a magical *'stone well.'* Yet the words tell us that, like Alice in Wonderland, she is *'falling / down, down, down.'* The enchantment of finding a brass-handled door above the *'water … dark and deep,'* leading into a *'crystal room / reflecting light / through /a rainbow prism,'* suggests a child's imagination for a fanciful escape. Alas, before the *'strange demonic eyes'* of the *'cat queen'* who *'reigns'* there, fancy quickly turns to nightmare, and *'a small child / kneels and begs / for permission / to leave.'*

The fluctuation of perspectives in the succeeding poems speaks to this same kind of disorientated, contradictory exchange between imagination and reality. Put another way, the poems – despite the "rainbow prism" of their manic energy – document psychological truths. In *a land with no weapons*, it is the fear of men that propels in her a *'desire to run / through the streets in the dark.'* In *eagle*, she is *'perched on a branch … an angel'* – safely out of reach, "empowered." In *transparent wings*, she is *'a moving target,'* wings *'flapping in distraction'* – until *'Cornered'* – her harm visible, *'Torn wings … one small drop of blood / staining / the jewelled net.'* Her fall is inexorable, and in her state of overwrought reality, the desperate hope of a last-minute escape merely assures it. In the penultimate poem, *head spinning*, she is *'plunging / diving into a deep, dark pond.'* The poem's abrupt ending – *'on a ladder … aerial view … spinning off'* – suggests a momentary loss of consciousness. When she "wakes," she will find herself "speaking" inside the slow and deliberate, very different world of *natural and man-made consequences*. She is now ensconced within the murky medium of the traumatic experience itself: "under water," below the *'cold, grey ocean'* she so much feared in *grey blanket,* having finally broken the surface of the 'deep, dark pond.' It is worth pausing to decode her speech in this crucial moment of passage.

Falling. Plunging. Diving. We note the rising degrees of intentionality in her "fall," assuming control at the point of entry. Despite the "gaps" in her new consciousness, it is she who has assumed the authority to speak in this "poem." She begins in the quasi-intellectual voice of an adult, questioning language; but soon identifies a different *'entry point ... the senses.'* What she sees, hears, and smells of *'bodily functions'* hints at a violation of her body. The loss of innocence is coupled with images of blood. Chilled to irony, her voice becomes that of a questioning child, knowing but not knowing. Her particular metaphor for the traumatic event can be found in the line, *'a stone was thrown into a deep pool.'* The "natural and man-made consequences" of this event are the ripples it leaves, which she likens to *'a thought / connecting / slowly / drawing circles / on the surface.'* As though to decipher their meaning (and cleanse herself), she chooses imaginatively or in remembrance to *'dive into the deep, cool water.'* But she is *'wearing / a big organ of / skin'* and the water is *'cold, wet, odourless / a bit like death.'* *'Coming up for air,'* she exclaims to her mother, *'There's something down there!'* Her fear of water, of falling into a *'deep dark hole,'* is now inscribed. Toward the end of this transitory flashback to the past, she discloses to herself an imperative for the future: *'I need to dive into a deep / dark pool / where there is no current.'* And she wonders, *'Will I come up smelling / of irises or daisies?'* At the end, she is *'dancing around the meadow,'* calling out to her mother, *'I can see you / you're in a circle / a circle / a circle / mummy / the stone has fallen into the / water and it is making circles / that connect with each other.'* Afterwards the fade-out – *'and then it all ... disappears.'*

Part 2: The Bodhisattva – At the still centre of the poetic whirl in Altered States is *the bodhisattva*, a poem that pauses to imagine a more realized form of altered state. It is a meditation or vision of an earthbound female figure, one who *'wanders through the streets / a heart as big / as the whole outdoors.'* Her mystic gift is a predisposition for *'rolling the dice / of compassion,'* in an engagement with life where the karmic formula for care (and self-care) *'equals Choice / equals Action / equals Identity.'* Philosophically, the figure of the bodhisattva embodies a spiritual concept for compassionate redress, healing the rift between self and world by a process of enlightenment. It is not surprising that the poet, as an alienated Western subject, would be receptive to Eastern forms of healing. As actually experienced by her, the bodhisattva is not a figure as such, but a synchrony of fortuitous events, each with a "miraculous" element. These different elements are the focus of the episodes that follow.

Asylum – Consequent to her breakdown, the poet enters an extended period of hospitalization. She first rejects the *'icepick'* of psychiatric questioning, *'hearing it / chip away at my spirit'* (in *after talking with Dr. G*). In *diagnostic roulette*, she resists *'labeling, re-labeling'* as *'tearing holes / in my shoddy identity.'* It is clear in other poems, however, that she finds opportunities in her medical confinement, beyond the respite and sense of safety in containment. Dreams, flashbacks, and carefully calibrated disclosures yield valuable insights. In *washroom*, she acknowledges a personal history of *'broken trust and faith.'* She is *'vomiting / up the past'* in *initial disclosure – dumping the self*. But of greatest consequence are those poems that reflect her sense of refuge and solidarity with the comrade ill. In small covens of shared pain and consolation, she identifies herself (in *the realm of belief*) as among the other *'manics, who can't sleep / like me,'* other *'monks praying for light.'* She participates in the *'collage of stories'* they share together, of *'abuses ... imbalances ... inheritances,'* collectively imagined in *a rainy Sunday* as *'tidal waves'* of personal catastrophe. From the standpoint of language, they are also *'wishbones in the throat.'* But the significant point for the poet is her sense of inclusion within a sheltered "community" of suffering. The personal invalidity and disesteem felt in the outside world is here suddenly transformed to its opposite: a place at the table, recognition, and a *voice*. In this first intimation of a miracle, we can say that the protagonist's sense of a wordless isolation ends. She can make an "image-story" of her *'volcanic anger,'* as she does in *the knife*; feel the pain and solidarity of others, *'vaporizing and slashing the air with knives'* (in *I am the universal child*); and acknowledge (in the closing poem, *a carpet of wet leaves*) the depth of her own wound.

Transference – The second evidence of a synchronous miracle unfolding occurs in therapy. There are two distinct phases. Responding to her psychiatrist's healing touch – a sympathetic, owl-like stare – the patient first recalls an emotional memory from her youth, suddenly unlocked from *'my robin's breast'* (in *melt down*) after being *'entombed' 'for 30 years.'* The suspension of the paralysis of feeling and the corresponding access to childhood memory, to the *'picked flowers / of the meadows / long ago'* (in *infatuation*), inspires and sustains a bond with her therapist. She is experiencing "transference," the unconscious displacement of past emotion to a present circumstance. A subconscious direction to the unreality of her attachment is to be found in the poem, *the owl and the pussycat*, whose title is borrowed from the well-known nonsense poem by Edward Lear. Beneath the shelter of her fancy, however, lies a serious purpose. The poet "recognizes" the therapist (in *a patient's love song*) as someone *'found … at the end / of a long / journey,'* a transcendentalist who will "see" her and listen. He is the embodiment of an idea both strange and familiar, *'from another continent / a comrade spirit / a healer.'* She divines his errand, therefore. In the ensuing therapy, his role as collaborator and compassionate witness to her pain will validate her experience. The effect will be greatly enhanced by the therapist's reliance upon her poetry as a primary mode of access to her inner states, expressed otherwise as a chaotic scatter of thought and feelings.

This is the second important event in the therapy. The resurgence of feeling in the first phase suggests that the phenomenon of transference is a temporary but necessary delusion, a safe harbour for re-fitting the sails of one's emotions. In this second phase, she is freed, therapeutically, to greater disclosure and insight into her painful past and turbulent, present emotion. In the poem, *possibility*, for example, the poet fantasizes killing as a way to *'put out the fire'* of her illness. Aesthetically, she enlarges the scope of metaphorical language already active in her notebooks. She luxuriates in this language to write her "inappropriate," yet exceedingly elevated, poems of "love" – poems, in truth, of *self-reattachment*. At an even deeper level, pertinent to the therapist's role as the "reader" of her story, poetic language is thus revealed as a therapeutic resource for her also: for the *transfer* of new meaning into her life, both present and past. Disabused of her initial, improper "transference," she leaves off *'whispering a / little song'* (in *the body as a temple for loving you*) and turns toward the greater *'surround of / movement and song'* in the outside world.

Stories – *'Pick up an old blue bone / tell your story.'* So begins *the circle*, the poem that opens this new chapter. What is striking in this poem and the others that follow (e.g., *let the sun shine in*) is the confident, positive tone in the poet's voice, *asserting* the value of telling one's story. In the elevation of her spirit, she apprehends clearly *'the human element'* in the stories of others, recognizing her sodality in *'a red trauma / reverberating around the world.'* In *I am white*, she shares some of the painful stories of her adult literacy students, refugees from other worlds. In *quilt by design*, the patchwork of shared experience that is *'women's work'* is understood as a project for *'recycling memories,'* an invitation to *'touch my pain / put the pieces together.'* It is also a cue to the author to tell her own story. Yet, more confidence is wanted. The outside world is still not a protected space. She is no longer inside the hospital walls, among confidants and friends who have similar stories. What extra step might be required? How will what is *inside* and understood intellectually be brought outside and experienced *emotionally*?

As it happens, coincident with her therapy, she was a student at OISE-UT. There, she came under the influence of mentors and new ideas, particularly as regards the value of personal stories, as the threadwork that binds and interprets a healthy community. Among the new concepts she learned were those of synchronicity and "flow." She was already *in flow* in her writing, with its immersive awareness of being "outside in" and "inside out." She would learn to transfer this same quality of "mindfulness" to action in the real world: to pay moment-by-moment attention to the living reality about her and to use her own personal vulnerability as an asset, to listen and to tell. Shared with other students, practiced through presentations or in the writing of her papers, this personal act of *valour* – of joyfully accepting risk – would become the third element in the miracle of her recovery.

Part 3: Mother – Confidence to meet the world becomes confidence to revisit her past. The matrix of confluent healing events – inclusion within a community of suffering, the disparalysis of feeling and compassionate witness to her story, and acceptance of risk in relation to action in the real world – has prepared the ground for the final stages of her journey. The golem (of trauma) has been replaced by *my guardian angel* (from Stories), conceived of as *'a harmony of body and soul,'* a powerful inner ally for comfort and self-affirmation, who *'speaks without words … comforts without touch,'* and whose silence is *positive*, not negative. Memories can now be safely rewound and imaginatively re-experienced. Afterward, she will return to the present to consolidate her healing. Reclusion and the talismans of nature – tree, cardinal, night sky – will play leading roles, as her spirit lifts toward reconciliation and forgiveness.

Memory – Mist is *'lifting off fields.'* A winding road, a river. A dream, an old photograph. The sound of rain. All seem to ask, *'where have I come from? / where am I now?'* The poems in this section are distinguished by a distinct clarity of vision and feeling for past events. A main theme is her quest to repair the sense of a "separation," first identified in *grey blanket* (in Prelude). Various prompts to memory enable the poet to *'focus / on my past,'* as she writes in the poem *mist*, but also to enter the past directly. In *the trunk*, she is a *'time traveller / going back, not forward,'* as *'precious nothings'* – a mauve button, the memory of a face painted on a boiled egg – take on a *'radiant meaningfulness.'* She is both present and not present, like a ghost visiting from the future. In the dream poem, *the brain: the back roads of my mind*, she sees *'a small child /*

playing by deep water' and wonders, *'could I / save the child? / would I / save the child?'* Though events are long past, she finds that *'everything is there ... the past is / the present / the present / flows through me.'* She is not merely remembering the past, but re-living it, *'digging deep / into fertile ground ... feeling the unfelt'* (from *ploughing the earth: a process of poetic transcription*). In *glamour puss*, her *'mind's eye'* recalls an old photograph, where she was dressed to look like a *'forlorn orphan.'* It causes her to remember why *'the cat has encoded itself in me,'* why she admired its independence of spirit, its *'beauty in line / beauty in elegant poses ... slinking around corners / to see what's on the other side.'* It is through such insights and acts of deep recall that she is able, ultimately, to re-integrate the past into present consciousness, in order then to leave the past behind, to separate from it in a normal, healthy way.

The theme of separation is revealed in unexpected ways as well. In *mist*, we learn that upon immigration to Canada, *'the family [that was] left behind / wept at the docks.'* The immigrating family, however, would find itself alone in its new world, and it may not be too unreasonable to suppose that the sense of separation and isolation would repose itself most deeply in the child least conscious of it. This disconnected, former life is the subject of many of the remaining poems. Father, mother, the Manchester background, the passage to Canada, her hometown of Antigonish – all are recalled. She does not omit the *'trinity of traumas'* – two will be revisited. But most striking are the poems that re-approach her parents. Conversations with her father form the basis for several. Each is remarkable for its level of affectionate detail. The poems reveal a diffident, gifted man with a taste for travel and a feeling for poetry, with "storytelling" memories of his own. The poet's tender regard is keenest, however, in the two poems of intimate conversation with her mother, *the button box* and *mother, other*. In the latter, the poet is the "other" of the title, close to – yet separated, lost, "invisible" to – her mother. These two poems are at the poignant heart of this episode of memory. The penultimate poem, *the dark angel*, is a dirge for the *'regrettably sad'* losses passed over by time – and for the lapse of time itself – when *'our curtain is finally drawn / our stories have been told.'*

Healing – The poet announces her decision *'to give up / the cloak / of victimhood'* and *'go home'* (from the opening poem, *Bev's tent and the magical toolkit*). The tent, her disembarkation point, is located at the bottom of a *'deep, dark pit,'* where she is encamped with a friend around a fire built from twigs, *'sparking imaginings of / primitive times.'* The toolkit is a *'bottomless ... bag,'* where *'a flashlight / a compass / a map ... whatever I need ... magically takes form.'* She will *'pull out / a book / of poetry'* before folding up the tent to *'climb out / of the hole'* (*'with the help / of each other'*). The setting for her journey home is, paradoxically, her home itself. Events occur there as acts of contemplation – in private moments of self-conversation, in rooms with "windows" to the world outside. Tellingly, the poems follow a seasonal pattern from winter to spring. At two in the morning, she recalls a red cardinal seen the day before, *'artistically contrasted to the / bleak surroundings ... a red lantern to light my way / along my path, in the darkness'* (from *the red cardinal*). It is winter. *'Gone are the French / white lilac blossoms'* of spring. In *Friday night*, frost is etched on her window in *'frozen rivulets / embedded / with stars / dazzling / from street lights ... branches / stiff, white / pointing / their fingers / telling / me stories / without words.'* Time and space – the seasons and the *'canvas / of urban / night sky'* – form the great surround and theatre for her healing progress, the frame and fixture for the poet's sense of a newly harmonized world.

The moon is her special confidant. In *the moon has a face* – from the Robert Louis Stevenson poem of the same name – the night sky reveals *'a clear night / a full moon / a face,'* surrounded by stars that *'look like twinkling diamonds / to me.'* With *'a crescent moon / hung around my neck,'* she imagines that she is *'standing / on the edge / of the world.'* In *the necklace (2)*, the full moon, a *'circle ... pale gold* within a *'glitter'* of night stars, offers her *'an aura / of protection,'* as if a talisman or *'token / of my / truer self.'* In contemplation of its *'gold-yellow sanded beauty'* (in *full moon*), she calls out to the moon directly:

'moon in the sky / connect me to the universe.' In these and other poems – in a gesture not quite gnostic but perhaps *transhuman* (the word is borrowed from the epic pantheist poet, Robinson Jeffers) – she puts herself at one remove from the pathos of existence, preferring instead the non-human, less compromised world of cosmic nature: of animals, trees, the colors and ornaments of the sky, and other hidden angels of the universe.

With the arrival of spring (in *spring*) comes a new awakening, when *'fresh, new / leaves / etch / the sky.'* The poet is experiencing renewal, notably using identical tropes to those from an earlier poem, *mother and child* (in Presentation), when notes of anxiety or ambivalence tempered *'the age old / story / of the universe / unfolding.'* Now new life is affirmed without demur. Cosmologically, the pivotal moment occurs in *changing sky*. Looking through the *'brown shutters'* in her living room, away from a book she is reading, she observes a slow kaleidoscope of colour in the early morning sky: *'baby pink / and 'powder blue,'* then *'just / for a moment … fluorescent grey,'* then – from the house across the street *'with its round / stained glass window / looking west'* – *'a bright yellow glow / a prayer'* (a moon, perhaps) – *'all of this / in the urban sky / at 7:30 a.m. / Sunday.'* An artistic angel, mildly psychedelic, has thus contrived to sketch her life in the tints of colour that surround her. A little housekeeping remains. Apologies are made, as in *I feel you beating* and *a daredevil with a broken wing*. In *the mermaid*, she confesses kinship with her *'sisters of the sea … hiding their tails / beneath the surface'* (to drown the careless sailor). In *cosmic crash*, she reconciles with an old enemy, seeing in a young man who collides with her at Toronto's Word on the Street, how *'his hazel eyes / sparkled / in the bright sunshine.'*

Home – Forgiveness and transcendence are the theme of this final passage. An important motif is her sense of a newfound stability. Water is no longer a threat. In the poem that gives the book its title, she salutes *the blue dragonfly*, whose invisible wings enable it to *'skim the surface'* of river and pond. *'I am a canoe,'* she says, *'knowing / trusting / the water / to hold me up.'* The attentive reader will notice that in the poem *transformation* she reimagines the whole history of her journey. As her metaphors rise to air, she is *'holding on to a butterfly's wing,'* experiencing *'flight above normal / renewal.'* The grey blanket of past trauma has turned to the *'burnt pink'* of a tranquil sky (in *the sky*). But the sense of an airborne, ravished, and sublimated self is most apparent in what is surely the apex poem of the collection, *atmospheric love*, where the poet has become *'my own guardian angel'* and the language of the poem itself even – chanting and ethereal – bears the stigmata of an ecstatic experience. Her last words are spoken to her mother – and to the *'eternal mother / conniving tributary peace strategies'* (from *mother*) – in a tender last greeting of farewell.

In these remarks, I have liberally threaded the explanatory framework with the poet's own words. This approach is meant to ensure a partnership between my exposition and the poet's voice as (together) we interpret *and elucidate* the poetry's dual purpose in this work: to deploy metaphor as a means of unblocking trauma and creating poetic speech in the first place; and secondly, through strategic positioning of the poems into episodes or "passageways," to allow the poet to tell her own story.

It remains only to identify a special quality in the poems themselves. We have noted their definite structure and evolved style, the brightness of their metaphor, the authenticity of the poet's voice. Yet there is something else. Hers is not a poetry that looks severely inward or is overly attentive to the self-conscious habits of literary form. She merely lets her arrow fly. Meaning is directed outward, using whatever linguistic resource comes to hand, in a poetry that is heartfelt and direct. Her voice is without artifice, unrestrained, "involuntary." There is, therefore, a great impression of speaking freely, in registers that range from the colloquial and prosaic to the vivid and elevated. The correct term for the special quality her poems manifest, or achieve without effort, is *charisma*. Words simply appear on the page, like emanations of spirit – lightly begun, as quickly robed and spun. An Unconscious slips into consciousness, a personality is rising on the page – and we look on.

The poems end the same way, with a kind of fluent finality. This speaks to the completeness of the poet's voice in relation to her experience. The poems self-organize into major themes, then into constituent parts, so thoroughly do they attend to the details of their complex story. For this reason, a poem can always be found to open or close a particular episode, with a clear sense of something beginning or ending, yet also following or leading on. This kind of open-ended closure is found within the genius of the individual poems as well. Through currents of metaphor and repetition, the poet guides each poem unerringly to the sense of its own ending, apt and complete in itself; yet irresolute enough to leave a thread for the next. At the bottom of the page for so many of the poems, one seems to find a closing charm – a protective amulet, a twinkling star – as if to light the way back up to the silence at the top of the page, and to the heaven above that.

Roger Langen – May 21, 2021

Biographical Note

Veronica Eley was born 1950 in Manchester (Middleton), England, the youngest of four children to Gordon and Mary (Carroll) Eley. The family moved to Nova Scotia in 1952, first to Dartmouth, afterward settling in Antigonish.

In 1974, the poet moved to Toronto. She was employed by the Toronto District School Board as an adult literacy instructor from 1994-2011. In 2002, she obtained her Master of Education degree from OISE-UT, an experience that was crucial – alongside therapy – to her "creative remembering" and recovery from trauma.

She retired to Dartmouth, Nova Scotia, in 2016.

Photo Legend

1. Poet as a young woman, ca. 1978.
2. As teenager, with cats.
3. Parents, Gordon and Mary Eley, 1940.
4. With dog, Pedro.
5. After the bar, with beau.
6. Wedding, 1981.
7. Young couple.
8. New mother.
9. Family.
10. In a mood.
11. The house on Sword Street, Cabbagetown, Toronto.
12. With her parents.
13. As adult literacy instructor, with some of her students.
14. As student, reading a poem.
15. With her mother.

NOTE – Photograph 2 – by Pauline Smith (Halifax) – reflects, visually, the poet's predestination to trauma recovery. She named the two cats, Black Thing and Grey Thing.

187

CPSIA information can be obtained
at www.ICGtesting.com
Printed in the USA
LVHW040352200422
716617LV00005B/318